Romantic Relationships and Sexuality in Adolescence and Young Adulthood

Romantic relationship formation and the engagement in sexual behaviors are normative and salient developmental tasks for adolescents and young adults. These developmental tasks are increasingly viewed from an ecological perspective, thus as strongly embedded in different social contexts. This volume brings together seven recent empirical studies that investigated different aspects of adolescents' and young adults' romantic relationships and sexuality, and the linkages with various characteristics of relations with parents, peers, and partners. These studies were conducted in six Western countries, including Australia, Belgium, Canada, Germany, the Netherlands, and the USA. Three studies examined the formation of young people's romantic relationships, and the other four studies focused on youth's developing sexuality. Together, they employed a diverse range of state-of-the-art research methods, including online questionnaires, computer-assisted interviews, daily diary assessments, and observations of dyadic interactions. In the editorial chapter, these recent advances in empirical research are discussed and framed within two important changes in the theoretical perspectives on young people's emerging romantic relationships and sexual activity: from risky behaviors to normative tasks, and from individual to contextualized processes. Throughout this volume, important directions for future research are suggested, specifically focusing on how to better incorporate the interrelational perspective into empirical research on these topics, and how to further bridge the gap between the research fields on romantic relationships and sexuality.

This book was originally published as a special issue of the *European Journal of Developmental Psychology*.

Daphne van de Bongardt is an assistant professor at the Department of Psychology, Education and Child Studies of the Erasmus University Rotterdam, the Netherlands. She multi-method research line focuses on biopsychosocial correlates of normative/risky/positive aspects of developmental patterns in adolescents' and young adults' romantic relations and sexuality, with a strong focus on different social contexts (i.e., families, peer relations, schools, media, festivals).

Rongqin Yu is a postdoctoral research fellow at the Department of Psychiatry of the University of Oxford, UK. Her research focuses on romantic relationship development, person-environment interactive processes, and the link with mental illnesses and violence.

Maja Deković is a full professor at the Utrecht Centre for Child and Adolescent Studies (CAS) of Utrecht University, the Netherlands. Her research area includes children and adolescent normative and deviant development, parent-child relationships, family interaction and effects of family-based interventions.

Wim Meeus is a full professor at the Utrecht Centre for Child and Adolescent Studies (CAS) of Utrecht University, and the Department of Developmental Psychology of Tilburg University, the Netherlands. His research area includes development of identity and personality in adolescence, personal relationships in adolescence, adolescent psychopathology, and longitudinal research.

Romantic Relationships and Sexuality in Adolescence and Young Adulthood

The role of parents, peers and partners

Edited by
Daphne van de Bongardt, Rongqin Yu, Maja Deković and Wim Meeus

Routledge
Taylor & Francis Group
LONDON AND NEW YORK

First published 2017 by Routledge

2 Park Square, Milton Park, Abingdon, Oxfordshire OX14 4RN
52 Vanderbilt Avenue, New York, NY 10017

Routledge is an imprint of the Taylor & Francis Group, an informa business

First issued in paperback 2018

British Library Cataloguing in Publication Data
A catalogue record for this book is available from the British Library

ISBN 13: 978-1-138-20991-6 (hbk)
ISBN 13: 978-0-367-07436-4 (pbk)

Typeset in Times New Roman
by RefineCatch Limited, Bungay, Suffolk

Publisher's Note
The publisher accepts responsibility for any inconsistencies that may have arisen during the conversion of this book from journal articles to book chapters, namely the possible inclusion of journal terminology.

Contents

Citation Information

The chapters in this book were originally published in the *European Journal of Developmental Psychology*, volume 12, issue 5 (September 2015). When citing this material, please use the original page numbering for each article, as follows:

Chapter 1
Romantic relationships and sexuality in adolescence and young adulthood: The role of parents, peers, and partners
Daphne van de Bongardt, Rongqin Yu, Maja Deković, and Wim H. J. Meeus
European Journal of Developmental Psychology, volume 12, issue 5 (September 2015), pp. 497–515

Chapter 2
Adolescents' relationships with mother and father and their links to the quality of romantic relationships: A classification approach
Sabine Walper, and Eva-Verena Wendt
European Journal of Developmental Psychology, volume 12, issue 5 (September 2015), pp. 516–532

Chapter 3
Gendered pathways to romantic attachment in emerging adults: The role of body image and parental support
Inge Seiffge-Krenke, Malte Persike, and Shmuel Shulman
European Journal of Developmental Psychology, volume 12, issue 5 (September 2015), pp. 533–548

Chapter 4
Adolescents' use of affiliative and aggressive strategies during conflict with romantic partners and best-friends
Jennifer Connolly, Kyla Baird, Valeriya Bravo, Benedicte Lovald, Debra Pepler, and Wendy Craig
European Journal of Developmental Psychology, volume 12, issue 5 (September 2015), pp. 549–564

Chapter 5

I get by with a little help from my friends: Examining the peer context of satisfaction with casual sexual relationships and experiences
Haylee K. DeLuca, Shannon E. Claxton, Elizabeth A. Baker, and Manfred H.M. van Dulmen
European Journal of Developmental Psychology, volume 12, issue 5 (September 2015), pp. 565–578

Chapter 6

Let's talk openly about sex: Sexual communication, self-esteem and efficacy as correlates of sexual well-being
Shawna Mastro, and Melanie J. Zimmer-Gembeck
European Journal of Developmental Psychology, volume 12, issue 5 (September 2015), pp. 579–598

Chapter 7

Parent and peer predictors of adolescents' sexual development: Can parents buffer peer influence?
Wim Beyers, Evlin Veryser, and Elke Verlee
European Journal of Developmental Psychology, volume 12, issue 5 (September 2015), pp. 599–612

Chapter 8

Project STARS (Studies on Trajectories of Adolescent Relationships and Sexuality): A longitudinal, multidomain study on sexual development of Dutch adolescents
Ellen Reitz, Daphne van de Bongardt, Laura Baams, Suzan Doornwaard, Wieke Dalenberg, Judith Dubas, Marcel van Aken, Geertjan Overbeek, Tom ter Bogt, Regina van der Eijnden, Ine Vanwesenbeeck, Saskia Kunnen, Greetje Timmerman, Paul van Geert, and Maja Deković
European Journal of Developmental Psychology, volume 12, issue 5 (September 2015), pp. 613–626

Notes on Contributors

Laura Baams is a postdoctoral research fellow at the Population Research Center and in Human Development and Family Sciences at The University of Texas at Austin.

Kyla Baird is a PhD candidate in the Department of Psychology, York University, Toronto, Canada.

Elizabeth Baker is a graduate student in the Department of Psychological Sciences, Kent State University, Kent, OH, USA.

Wim Beyers is a full professor in Developmental Psychology at Ghent University, Belgium.

Valeriya Bravo is a PhD candidate in the Department of Psychology, York University, Toronto, Canada.

Shannon Claxton is an assistant professor in the Department of Psychological Sciences, Morningside College, Sioux City, IA, USA.

Jennifer Connolly is a full professor in the Department of Psychology, York University, Toronto, Canada.

Wendy Craig is a full professor and head of the Department of Psychology, Queen's University, Kingston, Canada.

Wieke Dalenberg is a postdoctoral research fellow at Educational Sciences: Youth Studies at the University of Groningen, Groningen, the Netherlands.

Maja Deković is a full professor at the Utrecht Centre for Child and Adolescent Studies (CAS) of Utrecht University, the Netherlands.

Haylee DeLuca is a PhD candidate in the Department of Psychological Sciences, Kent State University, Kent, OH, USA.

Suzan Doornwaard is a postdoctoral research fellow at Interdisciplinary Social Science: Cultural Diversity & Youth at Utrecht University, Utrecht, the Netherlands.

Saskia Kunnen is an associate professor in Developmental Psychology at the University of Groningen, Groningen, the Netherlands.

Benedicte Lovald is a clinical psychologist and a former PhD candidate in the Department of Psychology, York University, Toronto, Canada.

Shawna Mastro is a PhD candidate in the School of Applied Psychology and Menzies Health Institute of Queensland, Griffith University, Australia.

Wim Meeus is a full professor at the Utrecht Centre for Child and Adolescent Studies (CAS) of Utrecht University, and the Department of Developmental Psychology of Tilburg University, the Netherlands.

Geertjan Overbeek is a full professor at the Research Institute for Child Development and Education, University of Amsterdam, Amsterdam, the Netherlands.

Debra Pepler is a full professor in the Department of Psychology, York University, Toronto, Canada.

Malte Persike is a senior researcher in the Department of Psychology, Mainz University, Mainz, Germany.

Ellen Reitz is an assistant professor at the Utrecht Centre for Child and Adolescent Studies (CAS) of Utrecht University, Utrecht, the Netherlands.

Inge Seiffge-Krenke is a full professor of Developmental Psychology in the Department of Psychology, Mainz University, Mainz, Germany.

Judith Semon Dubas is a professor by special appointment in Developmental Psychology at Utrecht University, Utrecht, the Netherlands.

Shmuel Shulman is a full professor in the Department of Psychology, Bar-Ilan University, Ramat Gan, Israel.

Tom ter Bogt is a full professor at Interdisciplinary Social Science: Cultural Diversity & Youth at Utrecht University, Utrecht, the Netherlands.

Greetje Timmerman is a full professor in Youth Sociology at the University of Groningen, Groningen, the Netherlands.

Marcel van Aken is a full professor in Developmental Psychology at Utrecht University, Utrecht, the Netherlands.

Daphne van de Bongardt is an assistant professor at the Department of Psychology, Education and Child Studies of the Erasmus University Rotterdam, the Netherlands.

Manfred van Dulmen is a full professor in the Department of Psychological Sciences, Kent State University, Kent, OH, USA.

Regina van der Eijnden is an associate professor at Interdisciplinary Social Science: Cultural Diversity & Youth at Utrecht University, Utrecht, the Netherlands.

Paul van Geert is a full professor (em.) in Developmental Psychology at the University of Groningen, Groningen, the Netherlands.

Ine Vanwesenbeeck is a professor by special appointment at Interdisciplinary Social Science: Cultural Diversity & Youth at Utrecht University, Utrecht, the Netherlands.

Elke Verlee is a psycho-pedagogical counsellor at the Centre for Student Counselling (CLB-GO), Deinze-Eeklo, Belgium.

Evlin Veryser is a counsellor in the MOBiL Crisis Team at the Saint-Camillus Psychiatric Hospital, Ghent, Belgium.

Sabine Walper is a full professor at the Ludwig Maximilian University, and Research Director at the German Youth Institute, Munich, Germany.

Eva-Verena Wendt is a postdoctoral research fellow at the German Youth Institute, Munich, Germany.

Rongqin Yu is a postdoctoral research fellow at the Department of Psychiatry of the University of Oxford, UK.

Melanie Zimmer-Gembeck is a full professor in the School of Applied Psychology and Menzies Health Institute of Queensland, Griffith University, Australia.

Romantic relationships and sexuality in adolescence and young adulthood: The role of parents, peers, and partners

Daphne van de Bongardt[1], Rongqin Yu[2], Maja Deković[2], and Wim H. J. Meeus[2,3]

[1]Research Institute of Child Development and Education (YIELD), Faculty of Social and Behavioural Sciences, University of Amsterdam, Amsterdam, the Netherlands
[2]Utrecht Centre for Child and Adolescent Studies (CAS), Faculty of Social and Behavioural Sciences, Utrecht University, Utrecht, the Netherlands
[3]Department of Developmental Psychology, Faculty of Social and Behavioral Sciences, Tilburg University, Tilburg, the Netherlands

The formation of romantic relationships and the engagement in sexual behaviours are considered normative and salient developmental tasks for adolescents and young adults. These developmental tasks are increasingly viewed from an ecological perspective, thus not only as individual processes, but also as strongly embedded in different social contexts, including the proximal social domains of parents, peers, and partners. This special issue brings together seven recent empirical studies on adolescents' and young adults' romantic relationships and sexuality in the context of relationships and interactions with parents, peers, and partners. In this editorial introduction, we describe two important recent changes in the theoretical perspectives on emerging romantic relationships and sexual activity: from risky behaviours to normative tasks, and from individual to contextualized processes. We then discuss recent advances in empirical research on romantic relationships and sexuality of adolescents and young adults. After that, we review the seven studies in this special issue, and discuss the contributions of these studies to the existing literature. Finally, we discuss directions for future research regarding how the interrelational perspective can be further incorporated into empirical research, and how the gap between the research fields on romantic relationships and sexuality may be bridged.

The first two authors share equal credit for this article.
No potential conflict of interest was reported by the authors.

The development of the knowledge, skills, and experience that are needed for the formation of healthy and positive romantic relationships and sexuality is a life-long process. Romantic feelings and sexual experimentation early in life form the building blocks for personal preferences and boundaries pertaining to emotional and physical intimacy, which are reflected back in more mature romantic relationships and sexual behaviours later in life (De Graaf & Rademakers, 2006; Joyner & Campa, 2006). Adolescence and young adulthood are particularly salient developmental periods for the exploration of romantic relationships and sexual behaviours (Collins, Welsh, & Furman, 2009; Tolman & McClelland, 2011). According to the ecological perspective (Bronfenbrenner & Ceci, 1994), which has become a dominant paradigm in the field of developmental psychology, romantic relationships and sexual experiences do not exist in a social vacuum. Rather, social contexts and interpersonal relationships with significant others (e.g., parents, peers, partners) contribute significantly to the processes through which adolescents and young adults shape their romantic relationships and their sexuality (Kotchick, Shaffer, Miller, & Forehand, 2001; Smetana, Campione-Barr, & Metzger, 2006). The aim of the current special issue is to advance the existing knowledge on how romantic relationships and sexuality develop during adolescence and young adulthood in the context of the proximal ecological social domains of parents, peers, and partners.

In this editorial introduction, we describe two important recent changes in the theoretical perspectives on emerging romantic relationships and sexual activities: from risky behaviours to normative tasks, and from individual to contextualized processes. We then discuss recent advances in empirical research on romantic relationships and sexuality of adolescents and young adults. After that, we review the seven studies in this special issue, and discuss the contributions of these studies to the existing literature. Finally, we discuss directions for future research regarding how the interrelational perspective can be further incorporated into empirical research, and how the gap between the research fields on romantic relationships and sexuality may be bridged.

CHANGING PERSPECTIVES I: FROM RISKY BEHAVIOURS TO NORMATIVE TASKS

Romantic relationships and sexual activities of youth have long been equated with risk. Early romantic involvements, especially those during the first part of adolescence, have been linked to various negative outcomes, including depression, anxiety, substance use, and delinquent behaviours (for a review, see Connolly & McIsaac, 2009). A particularly persistent finding has been that teenage romantic affairs that result in early marriage are generally associated with a higher risk for marital dissatisfaction and divorce (Whisman, Johnson, Li, & Robustelli, 2014). With regard to sexuality, adolescent (or premarital) sexual activity has traditionally been investigated as potentially dangerous and harmful for individual as well as public health (Fergus, Zimmerman, & Caldwell, 2007). This line of research, focusing on the risks involved in early relationships and sexual behaviours, has been of critical importance in light of the high prevalence rates of sexually transmitted infections (STIs) and unwanted teenage pregnancies (Finer, 2010; Forhan et al., 2009), and has yielded important knowledge about how to optimize prevention and intervention strategies that aim to promote youth's relational and sexual health (Connolly et al., 2014; Salazar et al., 2005). However, it tends to overlook the fact that early romantic relationships and adolescent sexual activity are not inherently risky.

Since last decade, the engagement in romantic relationships and emerging sexual activity are increasingly considered normative aspects of adolescent development and the transition to young adulthood (Collins et al., 2009; Tolman & McClelland, 2011). That is, romantic relationships and sexuality pertain to the expected behaviour patterns of adolescents and young adults, as evidenced by prevalence statistics from many Western countries. Concerning romantic relationship involvement, studies from Germany (Seiffge-Krenke, 2000), the Netherlands (De Graaf, Kruijer, Van Acker, & Meijer, 2012), Australia (Zimmer-Gembeck, 1999), and the USA (Carver, Joyner, & Udry, 2003) indicate that most teenagers in those countries have been engaged in one or more romantic relationships. Regarding sexual activity, in the USA (Martinez, Copen, & Abma, 2011), the UK (Mercer et al., 2013), and the Netherlands (De Graaf et al., 2012), more than half of the teenagers report having experience with sexual intercourse by the time they turn 18.

The "new" perspective on young people's engagement in romantic relationships and sexual behaviours, where these are considered as normative developmental phenomena during adolescence and young adulthood, has been increasingly utilized to guide a significant body of empirical work (for reviews, see Collins et al., 2009; Tolman & McClelland, 2011). In this growing line of research, scholars do not merely focus on potentially risky aspects of adolescent romantic relationships and sexuality, often followed by implications for how such behaviours can be prevented, but aim to better understand how the majority of adolescents' develop their romantic relationships and sexuality in a normative way. The resulting literature has accumulated important knowledge on how early romantic relationships and sexuality develop, and how to design effective comprehensive education programmes to promote healthy and positive relational and sexual development in youth (Kirby, 2008; Madsen, 2008). This change in perspectives on romantic relationships and sexual behaviours in adolescence and young adulthood from risky behaviours to normative tasks has guided empirical research to shift from an exclusive focus on identifying factors that may prevent youths from becoming involved in romantic or sexual relationships towards assessing factors that aid a more fundamental understanding of when, how, and why young people engage in romantic relationships and sexual behaviours. Also, it enabled the disentanglement of truly risky versus normative developmental trajectories, thus clarifying young people's different types of educational and health care needs.

CHANGING PERSPECTIVES II: FROM INDIVIDUAL TO CONTEXTUALIZED PROCESSES

According to the ecological perspective, which has become a dominant theoretical paradigm in developmental psychology over the past decades, changes in adolescents' behaviours, cognitions, and social relationships are the outcomes of continuous interactions between individual characteristics and socio-contextual factors, such as relations with parents and peers (Bronfenbrenner & Ceci, 1994). Consistent with this ecological approach, scholars have increasingly acknowledged that romantic and sexual developments during adolescence and young adulthood do not take place in a social vacuum (Smetana et al., 2006). As a result, attention for social contexts and interpersonal relations has become more prominent in the scientific study of romantic relationships and sexuality (for reviews see: Collins et al., 2009; Kotchick et al., 2001). Through this, valuable knowledge has been yielded about how developing romance and sexuality are linked to social contexts and interpersonal relations including parenting processes (De Goede, Branje, Van Duin, Van der Valk, & Meeus, 2012; De Graaf, Vanwesenbeeck, Woertman, & Meeus, 2011), peer norms (Van de Bongardt, Reitz, Sandfort, & Deković, 2015), and partner interactions (Aalsma, Carpentier, Azzouz, & Fortenberry, 2012).

The resulting body of literature has shown that parents, peers, and partners play important roles in shaping adolescent and young adult romantic relationships. In regard to the role of parents, according to attachment theory (Bowlby, 1982), adolescents construct working models of attachment, or mental representations of the self, and relationships, based on their relationship with their parents (Furman, Simon, Shaffer, & Bouchey, 2002). Adolescents subsequently use these working models to construct their later relationships with romantic partners (Furman et al., 2002). Empirical research provides support for these views (De Goede et al., 2012; Furman, Stephenson, & Rhoades, 2014; Seiffge-Krenke, 2006), showing, for instance, long-term positive associations between a secure attachment to parents and a secure attachment to romantic partners. Friendships also offer an important training ground for developing the capacities and expectations for later romantic relationships (Collins et al., 2009), as friendships and romantic relationships share various commonalities in that they are generally both voluntarily chosen, egalitarian, and based on reciprocity (Furman & Wehner, 1994). Consistent with social learning theory, longitudinal studies have shown positive linkages between the quality of adolescents' friendships (reflected in the levels of support, negative interaction, and power balance) and the quality of later romantic relationships (Yu, Branje, Keijsers, & Meeus, 2014). Furthermore, characteristics of romantic partners themselves, such as personality traits and self-esteem, also contribute to the quality of adolescents' romantic relationships (Collins et al., 2009).

In sexuality research, a consistent finding pertaining to the role of parents in healthy adolescent sexual development concerns the protective function of a high-quality relationship with parents. Adolescents who have a good relationship with their parents—characterized by high levels of warmth, closeness, and support—generally initiate sexual behaviour at a later age and engage in safer sexual behaviour (De Graaf et al., 2011; Kotchick et al., 2001). Concerning the peer context, a recent meta-analysis has shown differential relations between adolescents' own sexual (risk) behaviour and different types of sexual norms among peers (i.e., descriptive norms, injunctive norms, peer pressure, and risk norms), where adolescents' perceptions of descriptive sexual norms (peers' sexual behaviours) were most strongly related to their own sexual activity (Van de Bongardt et al., 2015). Regarding partners, it has been found that teenagers with more intimate relationships and who communicate more about contraception with their partner are more consistent in their contraceptive use (Manlove, Ryan, & Franzetta, 2007). However, the role of romantic partners in adolescents' sexual behaviours is still largely understudied, and deserves more attention.

CONTRIBUTIONS TO THE CURRENT SPECIAL ISSUE

The purpose of the current special issue is to expand the existing knowledge about how romantic relationships and sexuality develop during adolescence and young adulthood in the ecological context of interpersonal relations and interactive processes with parents, peers, and partners—three highly important proximal social domains (Collins et al., 2009; Smetana et al., 2006). To pursue a discussion on this topic, the current special issue presents seven empirical studies by scholars from six Western countries (Australia, Belgium, Canada, Germany, the Netherlands, and the USA), who have examined adolescents' and young adults' developing romantic relationships and sexuality in relation to various aspects of relations with parents, peers, and partners. Three studies examined the formation of young people's romantic relationships (Connolly, Baird, Bravo, Lovald, Pepler, & Craig, 2015; Seiffge-Krenke, Persike, & Shulman, 2015; Walper & Wendt, 2015), whereas the other four studies focused on youth's developing sexuality (Beyers, Veryser, & Verlee, 2015; DeLuca, Claxton, Baker, & Van Dulmen, 2015; Reitz et al., 2015; Mastro & Zimmer-Gembeck, 2015).

CONTRIBUTIONS EXAMINING ROMANTIC RELATIONSHIPS

In the first contribution, Walper and Wendt (2015) used a behaviour systems perspective and attachment theory to examine longitudinal links between various characteristics (i.e., relatedness, negative conflict, emotional insecurity, and dominance) of relationships with parents and romantic partners among German late adolescents. The authors found that various features of relationships with parents were predictive of romantic relationship features one year later. Relationships with mothers were more influential than relationships with fathers, with emotional insecurity with mothers being most broadly linked to all features of adolescents' romantic relationships later on.

In the second contribution from Germany, Seiffge-Krenke and colleagues (2015) analysed data from an 11-year longitudinal study to assess the impact of parental support and negativity and that of body image during adolescence on romantic attachment in young adulthood. They found that, for women, body image mediated the associations between parental support and fathers' negativity during adolescence, on the one hand, and attachment to romantic partners during young adulthood, on the other hand. For men, no such mediating processes occurred and only body image, but not parenting, was related to their romantic attachment. These results are discussed in the light of suggested gendered socialization processes.

In the third contribution, Connolly and colleagues (2015) investigated Canadian adolescents' use of affiliative and aggressive strategies during conflicts with best friends and romantic partners. Through observations of dyadic interactions, the authors found that female best friends were more affiliative than male best friends and heterosexual romantic partners. They furthermore observed gender differences in the interaction patterns within same-sex friendships versus romantic relationships. That is, within romantic couples, girlfriends displayed more mock aggressive behaviours, whereas boyfriends exhibited more affiliative behaviours.

CONTRIBUTIONS EXAMINING SEXUALITY

The fourth study of DeLuca and colleagues (2015) assessed over-time relations between various peer factors (peer sexual behaviour, peer approval, and peer communication) and American young adults' satisfaction with casual sexual relationships and experiences (CSREs) during Halloween, characterized as a high alcohol-consumption event in the USA. The authors found that more peer approval of CSREs was related to more satisfaction with the experience, both immediately afterward and at follow-up one month later. Yet, young adults who were more satisfied with CSREs immediately afterward were less likely to have told their friends about the experiences after one month. Furthermore, the link between the intention to discuss CSREs with peers and follow-up satisfaction with CSREs was stronger for young adults who engaged in non-penetrative sexual behaviours versus penetrative behaviours during their casual sexual encounters.

In the fifth contribution from Australia, Mastro and Zimmer-Gembeck (2015) examined cross-sectional relations between young adults' reports on communication about sex (frequency and quality) with mothers, fathers, and best friends, their sexual subjectivity (sexual body esteem and sexual pleasure self-efficacy), and their' sexual well-being, including sexual assertiveness, safe-sex behaviour competence, and affective responses to sex. The results showed that more frequent communication with mothers in high school and higher quality current communication with mothers and friends were related to higher safe-sex behaviour competence. Higher quality communication with fathers was related to more positive affect about sex. Sexual subjectivity, particularly pleasure self-efficacy, mediated various relations between communication and sexual well-being.

In the sixth contribution, Beyers and colleagues (2015) examined parent by peer interactions in cross-sectional data from a sample of Belgian adolescents. Specifically, they investigated whether parenting aspects (responsiveness, behavioural control, psychological control, and autonomy support) functioned as buffers for the relations between sexual norms among peers (descriptive and injunctive norms) and adolescents' own sexual behaviours. The authors' parents-as-a-buffer hypothesis was not supported by their findings. In contrast, positive parenting was found to strengthen the associations between sexual peer norms and adolescents' sexual behaviours; this was particularly true for late adolescents.

In the last study, Reitz and colleagues (2015) employed a multi-domain approach to investigate how individual, parenting, peer, and Internet factors were longitudinally related to Dutch adolescents' sexual behaviours. Specifically, they examined the effects of adolescents' levels of impulsivity, relationship quality with parents, and involvement with peers, and the time they spent on social networking sites (e.g., Facebook, Twitter), and interactions between these multi-domain factors. They found no significant interaction effects between the four domains, but significant main effects of all four domains while controlling for the others. The findings indicated that higher levels of impulsivity, involvement with peers, and time spent on social networking sites were related to more sexual experience over time, whereas a higher quality relationship with parents was related to less sexual experience.

STRENGTHS OF THE STUDIES PRESENTED IN THE CURRENT SPECIAL ISSUE

Each of the studies that are presented in this special issue has individual theoretical and methodological merits. We would like to highlight four aspects of this series of studies as a whole that we consider to be particularly valuable for the contribution they make to the literature on romantic and sexual developments during adolescence and young adulthood within the social contexts of relations with parents, peers, and partners.

ADVANCING A DEVELOPMENTAL PERSPECTIVE

Developmental perspectives suggest that romantic relationships and sexual behaviours typically undergo significant changes over the course of adolescence and young adulthood (Connolly et al., 2014; Zimmer-Gembeck & Helfand, 2008). The studies in the present special issue advances this developmental perspective on romantic relationships and sexual behaviours of young people in two ways.

First, the samples covered major developmental stages of romantic and sexual development, ranging from early (Beyers et al., 2015; Reitz et al., 2015), middle (Connolly et al., 2015), and late (Walper & Wendt, 2015) adolescents to young adults (DeLuca et al., 2015; Seiffge-Krenke et al., 2015), thus covering major developmental stages of romantic and sexual development. Furthermore, several studies specifically examined the effects of age on the roles that socio-contextual factors play in developing relationships and sexuality. DeLuca and colleagues (2015) found that peer approval of casual sexual relationships and experiences (CSREs) increased young adults' own satisfaction with CSREs only for the younger college subsample (±20 years), and not for the older non-college subsample (±26 years), indicating that the importance of peer approval for the evaluation of young people's own sexual experiences decreases with age. This result adds to the findings of a recent meta-analysis, which found that, across studies, the relation between peer approval of having sex and adolescents' own sexual activity was stronger in middle and late adolescence than in early adolescence (Van de Bongardt et al., 2015). Thus, whereas the importance of peer approval of sexual behaviours seems to increase towards the end of adolescence, the finding of DeLuca and colleagues (2015) suggests that this decreases again towards the end of young adulthood. This would be consistent with identity development theories, which propose that conformity to peer norms serves the need to identify and affiliate with peers for a sense of identity and well-being during adolescence (Newman & Newman, 2001). In young adulthood, however, this need tends to decrease after having developed a more autonomous sense of self (Berndt, 1979). Related to this, the moderating effects of age on the parent by peer interactions found by Beyers and colleagues (this issue) are also notable. They found that parental responsiveness and parental control affected the association between sexual peer norms and adolescents' own sexual behaviour only for older adolescents, and not for younger adolescents. Together, these findings illustrate that the developmental period from middle adolescence to middle young adulthood may be a particularly salient time for parents and educators to consider peer influences on young people's sexuality.

Second, four studies in this special issue used longitudinal data to address their research questions (DeLuca et al., 2015; Reitz et al., 2015; Seiffge-Krenke et al., 2015; Walper & Wendt, 2015), which permits the investigation of actual developmental processes over time. Over the past decades, scholars have increasingly employed longitudinal research designs to explore how ecological factors (e.g., individual characteristics, parenting processes, peer interactions) are associated with adolescent romantic and sexual development over time (for reviews, see: Collins et al., 2009; Zimmer-Gembeck & Helfand, 2008). The studies in this issue relied on data collected over relatively short (five days; DeLuca et al., 2015) to quite long (11 years; Seiffge-Krenke et al., 2015) time periods, with time intervals between assessments varying from one day to four years. As such, these contributions provide insight into how socio-contextual factors predict characteristics of young people's romantic relationships and sexual behaviours over short time cycles as well as longer developmental periods.

ADVANCING THE ECOLOGICAL PERSPECTIVE BY INTEGRATING MULTI-RELATIONAL CONTEXTS

Although the empirical evidence shows that parents, peers, and partners all play a significant role in developmental processes of young people's romantic relationship formation and sexuality, still, relatively little is known about how these social contexts operate simultaneously. The ecological model of human development (Bronfenbrenner & Ceci, 1994) not only distinguishes various contextual systems at the micro-level, but also considers that these systems interact with each other at the meso-level. The contributions to the current special issue advance an ecological perspective on romantic relationships and sexual behaviours of young people by investigating various social contexts simultaneously and comparing them as well as examining interactions between them.

The study of Mastro and Zimmer-Gembeck (2015) revealed that young adults who retrospectively reported more frequent communication with their mothers and best friends in high school reported greater safe-sex competence, whereas those who reported more frequent communication with their fathers reported more positive emotional responses to sex. In addition, Seiffge-Krenke and colleagues (2015) and Walper and Wendt (2015) both found differential effects of mothers and fathers on youth's romantic relationship quality. In the study of Walper and Wendt (2015), emotional insecurity with mothers was broadly linked to all features of adolescents' romantic relationship, whereas emotional insecurity with fathers was related to fewer characteristics of young adults' romantic relationship. Seiffge-Krenke and colleagues (2015) found that adolescents' body image mediated the association between paternal negativity (punishment and conflict), but not maternal negativity, and later avoidant romantic attachment. Together, these studies suggest that although mothers, fathers, and friends are all important social referents in shaping young people's romantic relationships, they may serve distinctive functions.

The current issue also includes two studies that examined interactions between social microsystems at the meso-level in relation to adolescent sexuality (Beyers et al., 2015; Reitz et al., 2015). First, Beyers and colleagues (2015) assessed how parenting practices interacted with (i.e., functioned as a buffer for) adolescents' perceived sexual peer norms in connection with their sexual behaviours. The observed parent by peer interactions add to those found in previous studies (e.g.,

Fasula & Miller, 2006), and emphasize the importance of considering how aspects of adolescents' relationships with parents and peers may create combined effects on how adolescents develop their sexuality. Second, Reitz and colleagues (2015) examined interactions between not only the parenting and peer domain, but also the increasingly important Internet domain in relation to adolescents' sexual behaviours. Although the authors found no significant interactions between these domains, such multi-domain models, which take into account these various social contexts of adolescents' lives and interactions between them simultaneously, likely tap into a more realistic representation of which factors are particularly important in comparison to one another.

STATE-OF-THE-ART RESEARCH METHODS

In addition to the longitudinal character of some of the studies' research designs, which are in and of themselves highly labour-intensive for both researchers and participants, the studies in this special issue used a wide variety of state-of-the-art research methods to collect their data, including online questionnaires (e.g., Reitz et al., 2015), computer-assisted interviews (CAPI and CASI; Walper & Wendt, 2015), daily diary assessments (DeLuca et al., 2015), and observations of dyadic interactions (Connolly et al., 2015). As such, these studies reflect that researchers increasingly use innovative research methods to collect data on the personal, private, and sensitive topics of romantic relationships and sexuality. It is to be expected that this trend will expand further, and that future research in these fields will continue to adopt e-based data collection techniques (through online or smartphone application surveys) and observational methods, both in experimental and in ecologically valid settings (e.g., dyadic interactions, social network sites such as Facebook, speed-dating events). Moreover, due to the transitory feature of adolescent romantic and sexual relations, studies using time-sensitive methods such as daily diary applications or intensive life relationship history recordings will help to gain more insight into the developmental courses of young people's romantic relationships and sexual behaviours.

A BROAD CONCEPTUALIZATION OF SEXUALITY

Another notable shift in the literature is reflected in the broad conceptualization of sexuality used in the contributions in this special issue. In all three studies that examined young people's sexual behaviour (Beyers et al., 2015; DeLuca et al, 2015; Reitz et al., 2015), a broad range of various sexual behaviours were measured, including kissing, touching, manual sex, oral sex, and vaginal and anal intercourse. Traditionally, in many studies, adolescent sexual behaviour has been conceptualized rather narrowly as heterosexual intercourse (e.g., L'Engle & Jackson, 2008; Meschke, Zweig, Barber, & Eccles, 2000). Although such an intercourse-focus fits with the risk-oriented approach of adolescent sexual activity–as intercourse can be seen as carrying the most potential risks for sexually transmitted infections and unwanted pregnancy–there are several disadvantages to this approach. Measuring adolescents' sexual behaviours as their experience with intercourse provides a limited reflection of adolescents' emerging sexual activity, as most adolescents follow a progressive sexual trajectory, and engage in non-coital sexual behaviours before they engage in intercourse (De Graaf, Vanwesenbeeck, Meijer, Woertman, & Meeus, 2009). Thus, this narrow approach excludes sexually active adolescents who have not yet engaged in intercourse, but who may have engaged in other (non-coital) sexual behaviours.

Furthermore, sexuality encompasses more than behaviours. Yet, in the literature, relatively little attention is paid to the investigation of cognitive or emotional aspects of young people's sexuality (Zimmer-Gembeck & Helfand, 2008). As a result, the reasons why adolescents and young adults engage in sexual behaviours or relationships (e.g., their own intentions and expectations) or how they experience and evaluate these relationships and behaviours remain less well understood. Increasingly, research is starting to move away from the behaviour-only focus by paying more attention to other aspects of sexuality such as emotions and satisfaction (Van de Bongardt, Reitz, & Deković, in press). This is also reflected in the contribution to the present special issue of Mastro and Zimmer-Gembeck (2015), who examined not only behavioural aspects (sexual assertiveness and safe-sex behaviour competence), but also cognitive traits (sexual body esteem and sexual pleasure self-efficacy) and emotional facets (positive and negative affective responses to sex) of young adults' sexuality. Together, these studies emphasize the relevance and significance of further investigating multiple dimensions (behaviours, skills, attitudes, emotions) of young people's sexual lives.

DIRECTIONS FOR FUTURE RESEARCH

The seven studies presented in this special issue contribute significantly to the existing literature on romantic and sexual developments during adolescence and young adulthood, and the knowledge about the role of social contexts therein. Building on their qualities, but also on some of their limitations, we observe four important directions for future research in these fields.

MOVING FURTHER: FROM RISKY TO NORMATIVE TO POSITIVE RELATIONSHIPS AND SEXUALITY

Moving beyond the increased recognition of romantic relationships and sexual behaviours as normative aspects of adolescence and young adulthood, instead of inherently risky, some researchers have begun to pay attention to positive outcomes of young people's romantic relationships and sexuality (Barber &

Eccles, 2003; Vasilenko, Ram, & Lefkowitz, 2011). For instance, being involved in a high-quality romantic relationship has been found to contribute to adolescents' feelings of happiness (Demir, 2008), self-worth (Connolly & Konarski, 1994), social competence and perceived popularity among peers (Furman, Low, & Ho, 2009; O'Sullivan & Meyer-Bahlburg, 2003), and provides an important new source of support in light of the weakening bonds with parents towards the end of adolescence (Demir, 2008). Whereas research on romantic relationships has a longer tradition of focusing on these positive outcomes, in sexuality research, recently, scholars have also begun to explore the positive aspects of young people's sexual behaviours. For instance, first intercourse experiences have been found to improve male adolescents' satisfaction with their physical appearance (Vasilenko et al., 2011).

Anchored in a growing acknowledgement of romantic and sexual experiences as having also positive qualities, such as social and emotional support and sexual pleasure, empirical evidence of how socio-contextual factors contribute to these positive outcomes is currently expanding. For instance, a recent study has found that a high-quality relationship with parents was related to higher global self-esteem of adolescents, which in turn was related to adolescents' experiences of more positive emotions after having sex (Van de Bongardt et al., in press). The contribution of Mastro and Zimmer-Gembeck (2015) in this special issue showed that communication with parents and peers about sex was related to young adults' positive affective responses to sex, partly through increased pleasure self-efficacy. Seiffge-Krenke and colleagues (2015, this issue) showed that parental support was associated with less avoidant romantic attachment in young adults. Building on these important findings, many positive aspects and outcomes of young people's romantic relationships and sexuality, and the role of social contexts therein, remain yet to be further investigated.

MORE ATTENTION FOR BIDIRECTIONALITY BETWEEN INDIVIDUALS AND CONTEXTS

Although scholars are increasingly employing longitudinal research designs to explore how socio-contextual factors are associated with romantic and sexual development over time (Zimmer-Gembeck & Helfand, 2008), most studies, including those in the present special issue, focus primarily on unidirectional socialization processes. That is, they generally focus on how social contexts affect adolescent romantic and sexual development. According to transactional theories, however, young people are not only influenced by social contexts, but they themselves, in turn, also select and affect their social environment (Smetana et al., 2006). In light of this transactional perspective, the theoretical and empirical emphasis on unidirectional socialization processes in the literature is problematic, as this underestimates the complexity of the dynamic relations between developments in young people's romantic relationships and sexuality, on the one hand, and developments in their social relations (e.g., with parents and peers), on the other hand. Several empirical studies have evidenced bidirectional relations between adolescents' sexual behaviours and parenting behaviours (Ream & Savin-Williams, 2005), perceptions of sexual peer norms (Van de Bongardt et al., 2015), and the use of sexualized media content (Bleakley, Hennessy, Fishbein, & Jordan, 2008). Hence, further advancing our theoretical understanding of bidirectional relations between social contexts and romantic and sexual development over-time, through the use of longitudinal research, is paramount.

MORE CROSS-COUNTRY COMPARISON STUDIES

This special issue encompasses seven studies conducted in European countries, North-America, and Australia, which largely reflects the general literature on young people's romantic relationships and sexuality, with the majority of the published studies focusing on Western developed countries. As a result, the existing empirical knowledge does not include the lived experiences of the 90% of the world's adolescents who are growing up in the "majority world", which includes Asia, Africa, Latin America, and the Caribbean (Raffaelli, Lazarevic, Koller, Nsamenang, & Sharma, 2013). This is problematic, as the norms and values related to adolescents' and young adults' romantic relationships and sexuality tend to vary across diverse cultural contexts (O'Sullivan & Meyer-Bahlburg, 2003; Seiffge-Krenke et al., 2010). At a socio-cultural level (across countries), adolescents living in more collectivist and conservative countries are generally more oriented towards their social context, more inclined to conform to existing social norms, and more sensitive to friendship-rules than adolescents in more individualistic cultures (Bond & Smith, 1996; Verkuyten & Masson, 1996). As such, romantic relationships and sexual behaviours of adolescents in more collectivist countries tend to be more strongly affected by parents and peers. A cross-national comparison (Li, Connolly, Jiang, Pepler, & Craig, 2010) between Canada and China revealed that a high-quality parent–adolescent relationship (characterized by trust, intimacy, and companionship) was negatively associated with adolescents' romantic relationship status and their romantic intention in China, but not in Canadian. Furthermore, Dhariwal and Connolly (2013) have suggested that adolescents in different cultural contexts may perceive different levels of autonomy from their parents regarding partner choice. The meta-analysis of Van de Bongardt and colleagues (2015) showed that, across studies, peer pressure was more strongly related with adolescents' own sexual activity in more collectivist countries than in more individualist countries. These findings highlight the importance of considering socio-cultural differences in how young people's romantic relationships and sexual behaviours develop in the context of relations with parents, peers, and partners. Specifically, more research on these topics in the "majority world" is paramount. Also, more cross-ethnic and cross-country research is needed to compare how various aspects of romantic relationships and sexual behaviours develop within parental and peer contexts, and how this differs across different socio-cultural contexts.

CLOSING THE GAP BETWEEN RESEARCH ON ROMANTIC RELATIONSHIPS AND SEXUALITY

To date, scholars in developmental psychology and related disciplines tend to focus their research either on romantic relationships or on sexual behaviours, and the literature in these two fields has proceeded relatively independently. This is striking as romantic relationships are typically the context in which the majority of adolescents' sexual behaviours occur (Manning, Longmore, & Giordano, 2000). Although several scholars have called for the investigation of young people's sexuality within romantic couples (e.g., Bouchey & Furman, 2003), strikingly, it is the research on sexual behaviours outside of committed romantic relationships ("hooking-up") that is expanding more rapidly (for a review, see Heldman & Wade, 2010). The contribution of DeLuca and colleagues (2015) to the present special issue, which focused on casual sexual relationships and experiences (CSREs), is clearly embedded within this line of research. Yet, up to now, much remains unknown about how characteristics of romantic relationships or romantic partners are associated with adolescents' and young adults' sexual behaviours and their evaluations thereof. Some researchers have started to fill in this gap, by examining sexual behaviours within romantic relationships (Maas & Lefkowitz, 2015; McElwain, Kerpelman, & Pittman, 2015; Welsh, Haugen, Widman, Darling, & Grello, 2005). Closing the gap between the literature on romantic relationships and sexuality will certainly advance both fields of research. Further investigating romantic relationships as a salient context within which many adolescents' and young adults' sexual experiences occur is therefore a highly relevant direction for future research. Closing the gap between the literature on young people's romantic relationships and sexuality will certainly advance both fields of research.

CONCLUDING REMARKS

Together, the seven studies in this special issue make a valuable contribution to the advancement of the empirical knowledge and theoretical understanding of how romantic relationships and sexuality develop during adolescence and young adulthood in the social contexts of parents, peers, and partners. Their findings, and the ecological perspective more generally, are also important for prevention and intervention strategies in education and health care that are aimed at promoting young people's relational and sexual health. By incorporating these insights into the salience of social norms, high-quality interpersonal relationships, dyadic interactions, and communication content and processes into such strategies, parents, peers, and partners may be valuable potential allies in the stimulation of responsible, healthy, and positive relational and sexual decision-making of adolescents and young adults.

REFERENCES

Aalsma, M. C., Carpentier, M. Y., Azzouz, F., & Fortenberry, J. D. (2012). Longitudinal effects of health-harming and health-protective behaviors within adolescent romantic dyads. *Social Science & Medicine*, *74*, 1444–1451. doi:10.1016/j.socscimed.2012.01.014

Barber, B., & Eccles, J. (2003). The joy of romance: Healthy adolescent relationships as an educational agenda. In P. Florsheim (Ed.), *Adolescent romantic relations and sexual behavior: Theory, research, and practical implications* (pp. 355–370). Mahwah, NJ: Erlbaum.

Berndt, T. J. (1979). Developmental changes in conformity to peers and parents. *Developmental Psychology*, *15*, 608–616. doi:10.1037/0012-1649.15.6.608

Beyers, W., Veryser, E., & Verlee, E. (2015). Parent and peer predictors of adolescents' sexual development: Can parents buffer peer influence? *European Journal of Developmental Psychology*, *5* (this issue). doi:10.1080/17405629.2015.1056775

Bleakley, A., Hennessy, M., Fishbein, M., & Jordan, A. (2008). It works both ways: The relationship between exposure to sexual content in the media and adolescent sexual behavior. *Media Psychology*, *11*, 443–461. doi:10.1080/15213260802491986

Bond, R., & Smith, P. B. (1996). Culture and conformity: A meta-analysis of studies using Asch's (1952b, 1956) line judgment task. *Psychological Bulletin*, *119*, 111–137. doi:10.1037/0033-2909.119.1.111

Bouchey, H. A., & Furman, W. (2003). Dating and romantic experiences in adolescence. In G. R. Adams & M. Berzonsky (Eds.), *The Blackwell handbook of adolescence* (pp. 313–329). Oxford, UK: Blackwell Publishers.

Bowlby, J. (1982). Attachment and loss: Retrospect and prospect. *American Journal of Orthopsychiatry*, *52*, 664–678. doi:10.1111/j.1939-0025.1982.tb01456.x

Bronfenbrenner, U., & Ceci, S. J. (1994). Nature-nuture reconceptualized in developmental perspective: A bioecological model. *Psychological Review*, *101*, 568–586. doi:10.1037/0033-295X.101.4.568

Carver, K., Joyner, K., & Udry, J. R. (2003). National estimates of adolescent romantic relationships. In P. Florsheim (Ed.), *Adolescent romantic relations and sexual behavior: Theory, research, and practical implications* (pp. 23–56). Mahwah, NJ: Lawrence Erlbaum and Associates.

Collins, W. A., Welsh, D. P., & Furman, W. (2009). Adolescent romantic relationships. *Annual Review of Psychology*, *60*, 631–652. doi:10.1146/annurev.psych.60.110707.163459

Connolly, J., Baird, K., Bravo, V., Lovald, B., Pepler, D., & Craig, W. (2015). Adolescents' use of affiliative and aggressive strategies during conflict with romantic partners and best friends. *European Journal of Developmental Psychology*, *5* (this issue). doi:10.1080/17405629.2015.1066244

Connolly, J., & Konarski, R. (1994). Peer self-concept in adolescence: Analysis of factor structure and of associations with peer experience. *Journal of Research on Adolescence*, *4*, 385–403. doi:10.1207/s15327795jra0403_3

Connolly, J., & McIsaac, C. (2009). Romantic relationships in adolescence. In R. Lerner & L. Steinberg (Eds.), *Handbook of adolescent psychology* (pp. 104–151). Hoboken, NJ: Wiley.

Connolly, J., McIsaac, C., Shulman, S., Wincentak, K., Joly, L., Heifetz, M., & Bravo, V. (2014). Development of romantic relationships in adolescence and emerging adulthood: Implications for community mental health. *Canadian Journal of Community Mental Health*, *33*, 7–19. doi:10.7870/cjcmh-2014-002

DeLuca, H., Claxton, S., Baker, E., & Van Dulmen, M. (2015). I get by with a little help from my friends: Examining the peer context of satisfaction with casual sexual relationships and experiences. *European Journal of Developmental Psychology 5* (this issue) doi:10.1080/17405629.2015.1044964

De Goede, I. H., Branje, S., Van Duin, J., Van der Valk, I. E., & Meeus, W. (2012). Romantic relationship commitment and its linkages with commitment to parents and friends during adolescence. *Social Development*, *21*, 425–442. doi:10.1111/j.1467-9507.2011.00633.x

De Graaf, H., Kruijer, H., Van Acker, J., & Meijer, S. (2012). *Seks onder je 25e. Seksuele gezondheid van jongeren in Nederland anno 2012* [*Sex under 25. Sexual health of Dutch youth in 2012*]. Delft, the Netherlands: Uitgeverij Eburon.

De Graaf, H., & Rademakers, J. (2006). Sexual development of prepubertal children. *Journal of Psychology & Human Sexuality*, *18*(1), 1–21. doi:10.1300/J056v18n01_01

De Graaf, H., Vanwesenbeeck, I., Meijer, S., Woertman, L., & Meeus, W. (2009). Sexual trajectories during adolescence: Relation to demographic characteristics and sexual risk. *Archives of Sexual Behavior*, *38*, 276–282. doi:10.1007/s10508-007-9281-1

De Graaf, H., Vanwesenbeeck, I., Woertman, L., & Meeus, W. (2011). Parenting and adolescents' sexual development in Western societies: A literature review. *European Psychologist*, *16*, 21–31. doi:10.1027/1016-9040/a000031

Demir, M. (2008). Sweetheart, you really make me happy: Romantic relationship quality and personality as predictors of happiness among emerging adults. *Journal of Happiness Studies*, *9*, 257–277. doi:10.1007/s10902-007-9051-8

Dhariwal, A., & Connolly, J. (2013). Romantic experiences of homeland and diaspora South Asian youth: Westernizing processes of media and friends. *Journal of Research on Adolescence*, *23*, 45–56. doi:10.1111/j.1532-7795.2012.00803.x

Fasula, A. M., & Miller, K. S. (2006). African-American and Hispanic adolescents' intentions to delay first intercourse: Parental communication as a buffer for sexually active peers. *Journal of Adolescent Health*, *38*, 193–200. doi:10.1016/j.jadohealth.2004.12.009

Fergus, S., Zimmerman, M., & Caldwell, C. (2007). Growth trajectories of sexual risk behavior in adolescence and young adulthood. *American Journal of Public Health*, *97*, 1096–1101. doi:10.2105/AJPH.2005.074609

Finer, L. B. (2010). Unintended pregnancy among US adolescents: Accounting for sexual activity. *Journal of Adolescent Health*, *47*, 312–314. doi:10.1016/j.jadohealth.2010.02.002

Forhan, S. E., Gottlieb, S. L., Sternberg, M. R., Xu, F., Datta, S. D., McQuillan, G. M., ... Markowitz, L. E. (2009). Prevalence of sexually transmitted infections among female adolescents aged 14 to 19 in the United States. *Pediatrics*, *124*, 1505–1512. doi:10.1542/peds.2009-0674

Furman, W., Low, S., & Ho, M. J. (2009). Romantic experience and psychosocial adjustment in middle adolescence. *Journal of Clinical Child & Adolescent Psychology*, *38*, 75–90. doi:10.1080/15374410802575347

Furman, W., Simon, V. A., Shaffer, L., & Bouchey, H. A. (2002). Adolescents' working models and styles for relationships with parents, friends, and romantic partners. *Child Development*, *73*, 241–255. doi:10.1111/1467-8624.00403

Furman, W., Stephenson, J. C., & Rhoades, G. K. (2014). Positive interactions and avoidant and anxious representations in relationships with parents, friends, and romantic partners. *Journal of Research on Adolescence*, *24*, 615–629. doi:10.1111/jora.12052

Furman, W., & Wehner, E. A. (1994). *Romantic views: Toward a theory of adolescent romantic relationships*. Paper presented at the Portions of this chapter were presented at the meetings of the Society for Research in Adolescence, Washington, DC, Mar 1992.

Heldman, C., & Wade, L. (2010). Hook-up culture: Setting a new research agenda. *Sexuality Research and Social Policy*, *7*, 323–333. doi:10.1007/s13178-010-0024-z

Joyner, K., & Campa, M. (2006). How do adolescent relationships influence the quality of romantic and sexual relationships in young adulthood. In A. C. Crouter & A. Booth (Eds.), *Romance and sex in adolescence and emerging adulthood: Risks and opportunities* (pp. 93–101). Mahwah, NJ: Lawrence Erlbaum Associates.

Kirby, D. B. (2008). The impact of abstinence and comprehensive sex and STD/HIV education programs on adolescent sexual behavior. *Sexuality Research & Social Policy, 5*, 18–27. doi:10.1525/srsp.2008.5.3.18

Kotchick, B. A., Shaffer, A., Miller, K. S., & Forehand, R. (2001). Adolescent sexual risk behavior: A multi-system perspective. *Clinical Psychology Review, 21*, 493–519. doi:10.1016/S0272-7358(99)00070-7

L'Engle, K. L., & Jackson, C. (2008). Socialization influences on early adolescents' cognitive susceptibility and transition to sexual intercourse. *Journal of Research on Adolescence, 18*, 353–378. doi:10.1111/j.1532-7795.2008.00563.x

Li, Z. H., Connolly, J., Jiang, D., Pepler, D., & Craig, W. (2010). Adolescent romantic relationships in China and Canada: A cross-national comparison. *International Journal of Behavioral Development, 34*, 113–120. doi:10.1177/0165025409360292

Maas, M. K., & Lefkowitz, E. S. (2015). Sexual esteem in emerging adulthood: Associations with sexual behavior, contraception use, and romantic relationships. *The Journal of Sex Research, 52*, 795–806. doi:10.1080/00224499.2014.945112

Madsen, S. D. (2008). Parents' management of adolescents' romantic relationships through dating rules: Gender variations and correlates of relationship qualities. *Journal of Youth and Adolescence, 37*, 1044–1058. doi:10.1007/s10964-008-9313-8

Manlove, J., Ryan, S., & Franzetta, K. (2007). Contraceptive use patterns across teens' sexual relationships: The role of relationships, partners, and sexual histories. *Demography, 44*, 603–621. doi:10.1353/dem.2007.0031

Manning, W. D., Longmore, M. A., & Giordano, P. C. (2000). The relationship context of contraceptive use at first intercourse. *Family Planning Perspectives, 32*, 104–110. doi:10.2307/2648158

Martinez, G., Copen, C. E., & Abma, J. C. (2011). Teenagers in the United States: Sexual activity, contraceptive use, and childbearing, 2006-2010 national survey of family growth. *Vital and Health Statistics. Series 23, Data from the National Survey of Family Growth, 31*, 1–35. Available from: www.cdc.gov/nchs/data/series/sr23/sr23 031.pdf

Mastro, S., & Zimmer-Gembeck, M. (2015). Let's talk openly about sex: Sexual communication, self-esteem and efficacy as correlates of sexual well-being. *European Journal of Developmental Psychology, 5* (this issue) doi:10.1080/17405629.2015.1054373

McElwain, A. D., Kerpelman, J. L., & Pittman, J. F. (2015). The role of romantic attachment security and dating identity exploration in understanding adolescents' sexual attitudes and cumulative sexual risk-taking. *Journal of Adolescence, 39*, 70–81. doi:10.1016/j.adolescence.2014.12.005

Mercer, C. H., Tanton, C., Prah, P., Erens, B., Sonnenberg, P., Clifton, S., ... Datta, J. (2013). Changes in sexual attitudes and lifestyles in Britain through the life course and over time: Findings from the National Surveys of Sexual Attitudes and Lifestyles (Natsal). *The Lancet, 382*, 1781–1794. doi:10.1016/S0140-6736(13)62035-8

Meschke, L. L., Zweig, J. M., Barber, B. L., & Eccles, J. S. (2000). Demographic, biological, psychological, and social predictors of the timing of first intercourse. *Journal of Research on Adolescence, 10*, 315–338. doi:10.1207/SJRA1003_5

Newman, B. M., & Newman, P. R. (2001). Group identity and alienation: Giving the we its due. *Journal of Youth and Adolescence, 30*, 515–538. doi:10.1023/A:1010480003929

O'Sullivan, L. F., & Meyer-Bahlburg, H. F. (2003). African-American and Latina inner-city girls' reports of romantic and sexual development. *Journal of Social and Personal Relationships, 20*, 221–238. doi:10.1177/02654075030202006

Raffaelli, M., Lazarevic, V., Koller, S. H., Nsamenang, A. B., & Sharma, D. (2013). Introduction: Special issue on adolescents in the majority world. *Journal of Research on Adolescence, 23*(1), 1–8. doi:10.1111/jora.12000

Ream, G. L., & Savin-Williams, R. C. (2005). Reciprocal associations between adolescent sexual activity and quality of youth-parent interactions. *Journal of Family Psychology, 19*, 171–179. doi:10.1037/0893-3200.19.2.171

Reitz, E., Van de Bongardt, D., Baams, L., Doornwaard, S., Dalenberg, W., Dubas, J. S., … Deković, M. (2015). Project STARS (Studies on Trajectories of Adolescent Relationships and Sexuality): A longitudinal, multi-domain study on sexual development of Dutch adolescents. *European Journal of Developmental Psychology, 5* (this issue) doi:10.1080/17405629.2015.1018173

Salazar, L. F., Crosby, R. A., DiClemente, R. J., Wingood, G. M., Lescano, C. M., Brown, L. K., … Davies, S. (2005). Self-esteem and theoretical mediators of safer sex among African American female adolescents: Implications for sexual risk reduction interventions. *Health Education & Behavior, 32*, 413–427. doi:10.1177/1090198104272335

Seiffge-Krenke, I. (2000). Diversity in romantic relations of adolescents with varying health status: Links to intimacy in close friendships. *Journal of Adolescent Research, 15*, 611–636. doi:10.1177/0743558400156001

Seiffge-Krenke, I. (2006). Coping with relationship stressors: The impact of different working models of attachment and links to adaptation. *Journal of Youth and Adolescence, 35*, 24–38. doi:10.1007/s10964-005-9015-4

Seiffge-Krenke, I., Bosma, H., Chau, C., Çok, F., Gillespie, C., Loncaric, D., … Rohail, I. (2010). All they need is love? Placing romantic stress in the context of other stressors: A 17-nation study. *International Journal of Behavioral Development, 34*, 106–112. doi:10.1177/0165025409360290

Seiffge-Krenke, I., Persike, M., & Shulman, S. (2015). Gendered pathways to romantic attachment in emerging adults: The role of earlier body image and parental support. *European Journal of Developmental Psychology, 5* (this issue) doi:10.1080/17405629.2015.1044963

Smetana, J. G., Campione-Barr, N., & Metzger, A. (2006). Adolescent development in interpersonal and societal contexts. *Annual Review of Psychology, 57*, 255–284. doi:10.1146/annurev.psych.57.102904.190124

Tolman, D. L., & McClelland, S. I. (2011). Normative sexuality development in adolescence: A decade in review, 2000–2009. *Journal of Research on Adolescence, 21*, 242–255. doi:10.1111/j.1532-7795.2010.00726.x

Van de Bongardt, D., Reitz, E., & Deković, M. (in press). Indirect over-time relations between parenting and adolescents' sexual behaviors and emotions through global self-esteem. *The Journal of Sex Research.* doi:10.1080/00224499.2015.1046155

Van de Bongardt, D., Reitz, E., Sandfort, T., & Deković, M. (2015). A meta-analysis of the relations between three types of peer norms and adolescent sexual behavior. *Personality and Social Psychology Review, 19*, 203–234. doi:10.1177/1088868314544223

Vasilenko, S. A., Ram, N., & Lefkowitz, E. S. (2011). Body image and first sexual intercourse in late adolescence. *Journal of Adolescence, 34*, 327–335. doi:10.1016/j.adolescence.2010.04.005

Verkuyten, M., & Masson, K. (1996). Culture and gender differences in the perception of friendship by adolescents. *International Journal of Psychology, 31*, 207–217. doi:10.1080/002075996401089

Walper, S., & Wendt, E. V. (2015). Adolescents' relationships with mother and father and their links to the quality of romantic relationships: A classification approach. *European Journal of Developmental Psychology, 5* (this issue) doi:10.1080/17405629.2015.1065727

Welsh, D. P., Haugen, P. T., Widman, L., Darling, N., & Grello, C. M. (2005). Kissing is good: A developmental investigation of sexuality in adolescent romantic couples. *Sexuality Research & Social Policy, 2*, 32–41. doi:10.1525/srsp.2005.2.4.32

Whisman, M. A., Johnson, D. P., Li, A., & Robustelli, B. L. (2014). Intimate relationship involvement, intimate relationship quality, and psychiatric disorders in adolescents. *Journal of Family Psychology*, *28*, 908–914. doi:10.1037/fam0000026

Yu, R., Branje, S., Keijsers, L., & Meeus, W. H. J. (2014). Personality effects on romantic relationship quality through friendship quality: A ten-year longitudinal study in youths. *PLoS ONE*, *9*, e102078. doi:10.1371/journal.pone.0102078

Zimmer-Gembeck, M. J. (1999). Stability, change and individual differences in involvement with friends and romantic partners among adolescent females. *Journal of Youth and Adolescence*, *28*, 419–438. doi:10.1023/A:1021612907073

Zimmer-Gembeck, M. J., & Helfand, M. (2008). Ten years of longitudinal research on U.S. adolescent sexual behavior: Developmental correlates of sexual intercourse, and the importance of age, gender, and ethnic background. *Developmental Review*, *28*, 153–224. doi:10.1016/j.dr.2007.06.001

Adolescents' relationships with mother and father and their links to the quality of romantic relationships: A classification approach

Sabine Walper[1,2], and Eva-Verena Wendt[1]

[1]German Youth Institute, Munich, Germany
[2]Ludwig-Maximilian-University Munich, Germany

Adolescents' relationships with parents are considered to be a major learning source and emotional base for developing expectations and styles of behaviour in close relationships. Using a longitudinal sample of late adolescents from nuclear families drawn from the German Family Panel pairfam ($N = 720$; mean age: 18.6 years), we investigated how adolescents' relationships with both parents influenced their romantic relationship quality one year later. Bagged (Averaged) Binary Recursive Partitioning was used to compare features of adolescents' relationships with mother and father (relatedness, negative conflict, emotional insecurity, and parental dominance) in respect of their importance in predicting similar aspects of romantic relationship quality. Overall, our findings suggest some degree of domain-specific continuities in adolescents' relationships with parents and partner, particularly for negative conflict, as well as more global effects for most features of the parent–adolescent relationship. Emotional insecurity with mother was most broadly linked to all features of adolescents' romantic relationship. Overall, adolescents' relationship with mother was found to be more influential than their relationship with father. The findings are discussed with reference to a behavioural systems perspective and attachment theory.

We thank Dr. Ulrich Pötter for conducting the statistical analyses, Christina Gschwendtner for preparatory work, Xuan Li for careful language checks, and, last but not least, all participants of the pairfam panel.

No potential conflict of interest was reported by the authors.

This research was supported by a grant of the German Research Foundation to the first author (Wa 949/11-1 through 3) as co-principle investigator of the German Family Panel pairfam at the Ludwig-Maximilian-University, Munich. This paper uses data from the pairfam panel, coordinated by Josef Brüderl, Karsten Hank, Johannes Huinink, Bernhard Nauck, Franz Neyer, and Sabine Walper. pairfam is funded as a long-term project by the German Research Foundation (DFG).

During the past two decades, increasing attention has been paid to adolescents' and young adults' romantic relationships (Collins, Welsh, & Furman, 2009). Romantic development up to late adolescence involves a variety of processes which not only comprise an increase in romantic experiences, but also support a more advanced quality of these relationships as reflected in higher intimacy and commitment (Collins et al., 2009; Connolly & Goldberg, 1999). With increasing stability, these relationships are also more likely to serve the functions of an attachment relationship as a "safe haven" in times of personal stress and as a "secure base" from which one explores and confronts challenging tasks (Collins & Feeney, 2000; Furman & Wehner, 1997; Seiffge-Krenke, 2003). Furthermore, while balancing relatedness with individual needs for autonomy is a salient issue throughout development, achieving autonomy along with intimacy in romantic relationships is particularly relevant to advanced stages of partnership development (Taradash, Connolly, Pepler, Craig, & Costa, 2001). Thus, understanding romantic development requires a broad framework that incorporates multiple relationship features.

While adolescents' romantic involvement marks a major step in the longer process of developing affective ties beyond the family of origin, parents continue to remain important. In fact, a wealth of research has demonstrated the long-term influence of resources and relationship experiences in the family of origin on later romantic relationships (e.g., Collins et al., 2009; Conger, Cui, Bryant, & Elder, 2000; Darling, Cohan, Burns, & Thompson, 2008; Seiffge-Krenke, Overbeek, & Vermulst, 2010). A comprehensive perspective is offered by the development of early adult romantic relationships model (DEARR; Bryant & Conger, 2002). This model posits that the quality of interactions among family members, parenting style, family stability, and socio-economic resources of the family of origin jointly influence how young adults think, behave and feel about intimate relationships and their significant other (see also Conger et al., 2000).

Within this broad picture, theoretical perspectives on parenting (e.g., Conger et al., 2000), attachment (e.g., Furman & Wehner, 1994) and individuation (e.g., Saraiva & Matos, 2012; Youniss & Smollar, 1985) have each proposed distinct feature of parent–adolescent relationships as important predictors of romantic development. While each of these approaches claims broad relevance for explaining a wide range of outcomes, domain-specific views on socialization in the family (Grusec & Davidov, 2010) as well as the behavioural systems perspective (Furman & Wehner, 1994) emphasize distinct functions of each domain of family socialization, suggesting specific links among similar features of relationships with parents and partner. Such domain-specific continuities have been pointed out for links between the interparental relationship and late adolescents' romantic relationships with respect to aggression as well as relationship satisfaction (Hare, Miga, & Allen, 2009), but are less clear with respect to features of the parent–adolescent relationship.

Building on these approaches, the present paper addresses four major dimensions of relationship experiences with parents (relatedness, negative conflict, emotional insecurity, and parental dominance), explores their links to similar aspects of romantic relationship quality, and compares mothers' and fathers' contribution. Special attention is paid to how broadly certain features of adolescents' relationship quality with parents matter, and whether constellations of relationship features, rather than isolated dimensions of parent–adolescent relationships, are most impactful.

HOW THE PARENT–CHILD RELATIONSHIP AFFECTS ADOLESCENTS' ROMANTIC RELATIONSHIPS

Influences of parenting and conflict with parents. Several studies have found that adolescents and young adults with accepting and involved parents reported higher quality of romantic relationships, e.g., increased mutuality (Auslander, Short, Succop, & Rosenthal, 2009), higher connectedness, less discord, more functional conflict resolution (Crockett & Randall, 2006), and higher relationship satisfaction (Conger et al., 2000), suggesting continuity of positive and negative behaviours in close relationships. Based on longitudinal data across a 15-year span, Conger et al. (2000) showed that young adolescents who experienced nurturant-involved parenting later displayed more warm and supportive behaviour towards their romantic partner in young adulthood, which further contributed to higher relationship satisfaction. In contrast, adolescents who had experienced negative reciprocity with parents evidenced similar negative emotionality in romantic relationships in early adulthood (Crockett & Randall, 2006; Reese-Weber & Kahn, 2005). Overall, these findings suggest more global influences of positive relationship experiences with parents on (later) romantic relationships (Conger et al., 2000), while dysfunctional conflict styles may evidence more specific continuity (Crockett & Randall, 2006).

Influences of attachment experiences. Attachment theory foregrounds emotional security as a major resource in self-regulation and coping with stress, which is facilitated by responsive parenting and guides expectations and behaviour in close relationships. Many findings suggest that an insecure attachment style with parents, resulting from insensitive and unresponsive parenting in childhood, is likely to spill over into romantic relationships (e.g., Duemmler & Kobak, 2001; Grossmann, Grossmann, Winter, & Zimmermann, 2002). Roisman, Collins, Sroufe, and Egeland (2005) found that young adults who were securely attached to their primary caregivers in infancy showed higher observed partnership quality than those with insecure attachment, and evidenced more secure attachment representations regarding their romantic partner, mediated by more positive perceptions of their partner. Conversely, insecure attachment with parents and peers in adolescence was found relevant to anxious romantic attachment in adulthood (Pascuzzo, Cyr, & Moss, 2013). During adolescence, insecurity with mother predicted increases in insecurity with romantic partner across two years (Doyle, Lawford, & Markiewicz, 2009). Furthermore, secure attachment representations were found to buffer romantic relationship quality against the transmission of interparental aggression (Hare et al., 2009). Overall, these findings suggest domain-specific continuity as well as more global effects.

Individuation and romantic development. Adolescence brings about changes in parent–child relationships which reflect adolescents' increasing demands for autonomy (Seiffge-Krenke et al., 2010). As pointed out by individuation theory, families who successfully adapt to these demands and manage to maintain high relatedness while granting more autonomy provide the most favourable conditions for adolescents' individuation as a resource for their personal and social development (Youniss & Smollar, 1985). Studies using typological approaches which combine indicators of relatedness and autonomy demonstrated the advantages of healthy or secure individuation for adolescents' adjustment (Kruse & Walper, 2008; McClanahan & Holmbeck, 1992) as well as for the quality of romantic relationships as evident in high emotional security and low engulfment anxiety (Saraiva & Matos, 2012). In line with attachment theory, emotional security with parents was most strongly linked to emotional security with partner. Focusing specifically adolescents' autonomy in their romantic relationships, autonomy but not intimacy with mother was found relevant, even beyond the stronger contribution of autonomy with friends (Taradash et al., 2001). This may suggest more domain-specific continuity of autonomy with parents and partner.

Gender issues. Only a few studies have compared the role of mothers and fathers or considered adolescents' gender as moderating factors. Reese-Weber and Kahn (2005) found that adolescents' conflict style with the mother was more directly linked to later conflict resolution with romantic partners than their conflict style with the father. Similarly, a longitudinal study across adolescence showed that a positive trajectory of the mother–adolescent relationship was more consistently associated with later connectedness with the romantic partner than a similar trajectory of father–adolescent relationships (Seiffge-Krenke et al., 2010). Anxious love, however, was only predicted by adolescents' distant relationship trajectory with the father. Investigating girls only, Scharf and Mayseless (2008) reported that a better quality of adolescents' relationship with mother predicted a later start of sexual activities, whereas both the quality of the mother–adolescent relationship and the father–adolescent relationship were linked to better romantic relationship quality.

Research questions. This paper has three major aims. First, we investigate how four features of parent–adolescent relationships (relatedness, negative conflict, emotional insecurity, and parental dominance) are linked to similar features in late adolescents' romantic relationships one year later. Specifically, we ask whether certain links between adolescents' relationships with parents and partners are confined to similar features (domain-specific continuity), as suggested by previous findings for negative conflict and autonomy, and whether other features of the parent–adolescent relationship are linked to many features of the romantic relationship (global effect). Since conceptions of parenting, attachment and individuation jointly emphasize the role of relatedness, and in light of available evidence, relatedness with parents is expected to indicate global effects. Furthermore, given the key role of emotional security as a resource for interpersonal competence outlined in attachment research, global effects are also expected for emotional insecurity with parents. Secondly, in order to examine the typological assumptions of attachment and individuation theories, we adopt a classification approach, which tests not only the main effects but also the interactions between predictor variables. According to attachment theory, low emotional insecurity combined with high relatedness represents secure attachment, suggesting that this constellation should be most beneficial. Regarding individuation theory, high autonomy (represented by low parental dominance) combined with high relatedness indicates successful individuation; hence both dimensions may jointly prove particularly important. Inspecting interaction effects also allows testing any moderation effects of emotional insecurity (Hare et al., 2009) as well as the salience of same- and opposite-sex parents. Finally, we compare the respective contributions of adolescents' relationship to mother and father, assuming that adolescents' relationship with mother is more predictive of romantic relationship quality than the father–adolescent relationship.

METHOD

Sample

Data for the present study were drawn from the adolescent cohort (born 1991–1993) of the German Family Panel pairfam (www.pairfam.de/en; Huinink et al., 2011). The representative sample was drawn from register data and participants were interviewed annually since 2008/2009 using computer-assisted personal interviews as well as self-administered computer-based assessments. Our analyses were based on longitudinal data from wave 2 (2009/2010) and wave 3 (2010/2011). The sample was restricted to adolescents currently living with both biological parents ($n = 1.981$; 66.0% of the longitudinal sample), and among these to adolescents who were involved with a romantic partner in wave 3 (36.3%, $n = 720$; average relationship duration: 14.5 months, $SD = 11.8$; mean age: 18.61 years, $SD = 0.86$; 42.4% male).

Measures

Four aspects of adolescents' relationships with parents and partner were included: relatedness, negative conflict, emotional insecurity, and parental dominance versus autonomy with partner. Identical indicators were available for relationship quality with mother and father, and similar indicators were constructed for the partner relationship. All items were answered using a 5-point rating, and all scales showed adequate internal consistency (Cronbach's alpha = .68–.83). Detailed information on (sub)scales and items is provided in Table 1 and documented online (see Thönnissen et al., 2014).

Adolescents' relationship with mother and father. The *Relatedness* scale included two subscales measuring positive parental regard (Admiration) and adolescents' self-disclosure (Intimacy), each comprising two items adapted from the Network of Relationships Inventory (NRI; Furman & Buhrmester, 1985). The *Negative Conflict* scale comprised four items, including two items on conflict frequency (adapted from the NRI) and two on negative parental communication (from Olson et al., 1983). The scale indicating *Emotional Insecurity* in relation to parents combined two subscales measuring ambivalence and fear of love withdrawal, which were adapted from the Munich Individuation Test of Adolescence (MITA, see Kruse & Walper, 2008). Finally, two single-item indicators of *Parental Dominance* and *Compliance* were included. Both items were adapted from the NRI-scale Dominance, but correlated only weakly ($r < .20$), so they were used as separate predictors.

Adolescents' romantic relationship quality. Four indicators were used to assess the quality of romantic relationships at t3 (see Table 1). *Relatedness* was measured by similar scales as used for adolescents' relationships with parents. *Negative Conflict* included information on the frequency of conflict (adapted from the NRI) and on self-reported verbal aggression and withdrawal as conflict style with the partner (cf. Thönnissen et al., 2014). *Emotional Insecurity* in the partnership was measured similarly as for parents (using the subscales Fear of Love Withdrawal and Ambivalence of the MITA). *Autonomy* was assessed using four items from the Couple Climate Scales (Schneewind & Kruse, 2002).

Control variables. To control for contextual factors highlighted in the DEARR model, we included a 3-item scale on perceived *Economic Deprivation* (adapted from Walper, 2009) assessed at wave 2 (Cronbach's alpha = .84; $M = 2.09$, SD = .92, sample item: "My parents often have to forego something because they have to watch their budget."), as well as the level of adolescent's *School Education* (wave 3) defined by type of school track targeting vocational or academic training (low, medium, and high). Finally, we controlled for duration of the romantic relationship (in months), age (in years) and gender. Correlations of all indicators are documented in the appendix.

Analyses

We chose Bagged (Averaged) Binary Recursive Partitioning (sometimes nicknamed "Random Forests") as a semi-parametric classification tool (see Merkle & Shaffer, 2011; Strobl, Malley, & Tutz, 2009). Compared with more

TABLE 1

Indicators of adolescents' relationship quality with mother/father (t2) and romantic partner (t3).

Indicators	*Subscales (number of items)*	*Sample items*	*Number of items*	*Cronbach's alpha M (SD)*	
Relationship quality with mother/father (t2)					
				Mother	*Father*
Relatedness	Intimacy (2) Admiration (2)	How often do you share your secrets and private feelings with your mother/your father?	4	.78 3.58 (0.70)	.78 3.23 (0.70)
Emotional insecurity	Fear of love withdrawal (3) Ambivalence (3)	When I made a mistake I wonder if my mother/ my father still likes me.	6	.75 1.83 (0.72)	.83 1.87 (0.82)
Negative conflict	Conflict frequency (2) Negative communication (2)	How often do you and your mother/your father disagree and quarrel?	4	.79 2.46 (0.73)	.80 2.39 (0.75)
Parental dominance	–	How often does your mother/your father get her/his way when you can't agree on something?	1	– 3.21 (0.88)	– 3.31 (0.92)
Compliance	–	How often does your mother/your father make you do things her/his way?	1	– 2.96 (0.88)	
Relationship quality with romantic partner (t3)				*Partner*	
Relatedness	Intimacy (2) Admiration (2)	How often do you share your secrets and private feelings with [name of current partner]?	4	.68 4.10 (0.53)	
Emotional insecurity	Fear of love withdrawal (3) Ambivalence (2)	When I disappoint or annoy [name of current partner], I am afraid that he/she won't like me anymore.	5	.75//1.87 (0.74)	
Negative conflict	Conflict frequency (2) Verbal aggression (2) Withdrawal (2)	How often do you and [name of current partner] disagree and quarrel?	6	.77 2.15 (0.67)	
Autonomy	In our partnership I can follow my own interests without [name of current partner] getting upset		4	.75 3.77 (.75)	

classical procedures, regression forests are better able to deal with large numbers of predictors (here 15) and collinearities, and to provide estimates of non-linear effects and variable importance. The method is consistent in the presence of interaction or indirect effects. This is in remarkable contrast to methods based on classical least squares methods that typically result in biased relative importance measures. Furthermore, the method provides consistent estimates of classification accuracy based on classification errors in subsamples not used for model fitting.

The main building block of the random forest methodology is the construction of a recursive partitioning (a recursive splitting of the data along the values of a single covariate, i.e. the building of a tree). A typical example of tree analysis is provided in Figure 1, depicting the predictors of emotional insecurity with partner. Emotional insecurity with mother contributed to several splits (nodes 1, 5, and 9), proving most important (split at node 1). In this

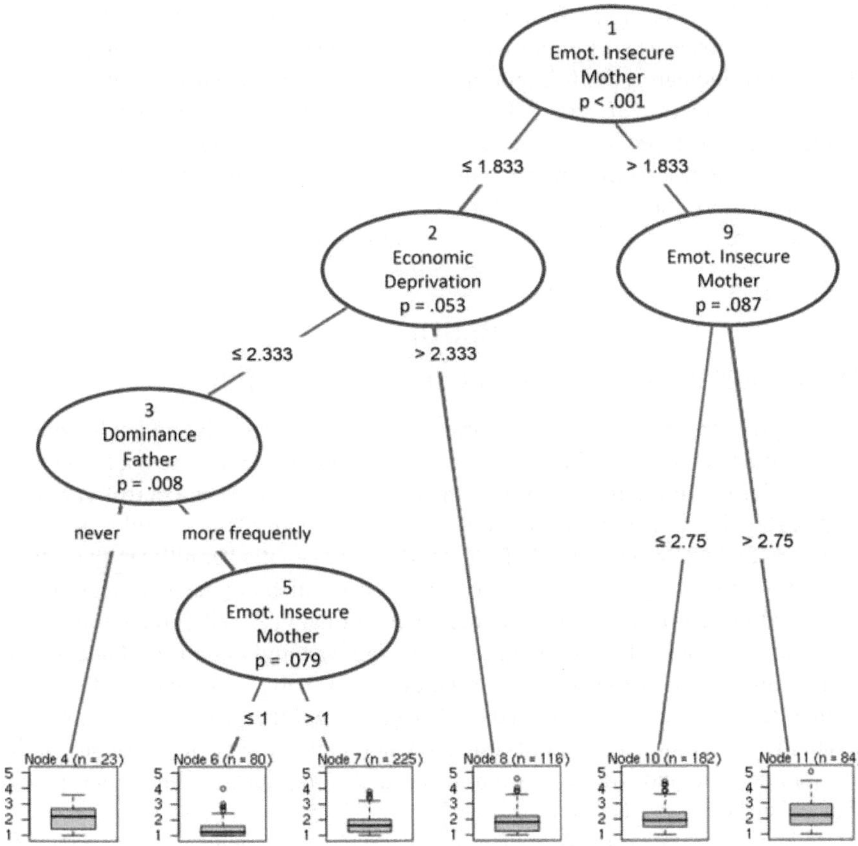

Figure 1. Sample tree predicting emotional insecurity with romantic partner.

example, economic deprivation and paternal dominance also contributed to the outcome variable.

However, single-tree analyses lack stability, do not work well in the presence of interaction effects, and typically provide only limited insight into interactions or non-linearities. Random forests generalize the method by repeatedly building trees based on random subsets of the data and random subsets of covariates. This makes it possible to consistently assess the role of covariates for the prediction of outcomes even in cases where their influence is masked by other covariates or by influential or outlying data subsets. Aggregation of the results across the 2000 tree analyses allows gauging the relative importance of covariates as well as estimating non-linear and interaction effects. The reported importance measures did not result from a covariate selection procedure, but the aggregated results were based upon models including all covariates. "Importance of a covariate" in the context of random forests is based on the average tree depth of the first appearance of a split based on that covariate within a tree.

All calculations were performed using R (R Core Team, 2015). In reporting the findings, we inspected Minimal Depth as an indicator of predictive importance (low values indicating high importance), examined the linearity of effects, and addressed interaction effects. All analyses were controlled for adolescents' age, gender, school type, economic deprivation, and duration of the romantic relationship. Partnership duration was included to disentangle the effects of age and partnership duration and explore differences in the importance of parent–adolescent relationships in short- and long-term romantic relationships.

RESULTS

The importance of predictors: Inspecting depth

Table 2 provides an overview of the importance of predictors based on the rank of their minimal depth, the value of their minimal depth (in parentheses) and a cut-off criterion based on the mean variable importance measure. The control variables relationship duration and age were linked to all four dependent variables, whereas gender differences emerged only for autonomy and negative conflict with partner. Emotional insecurity with mother contributed to all outcome variables, while emotional insecurity with father predicted emotional insecurity and autonomy in the romantic relationship. Relatedness to mother was important for relatedness as well as autonomy in the romantic relationship. Finally, negative conflict with mother and with father both predicted negative conflict with partner. Neither economic deprivation and school education, nor relatedness to father, or any of the four single-item indicators of dominance and compliance with either parent showed sufficient predictive power.

Highest importance (rank 1 of minimal depth) was found for the impact of relationship duration on relatedness and negative conflict with partner.

TABLE 2
Effects of predictors on adolescents' relationship quality with romantic partner: rank order of minimal depth and absolute values of minimal depth (in parentheses) derived from bagged (averaged) binary recursive partitioning analyses.

	Relationship quality with romantic partner			
Predictors	*Relatedness*	*Negative conflict*	*Emotional insecurity*	*Autonomy*
Age	2 (2.28)	2 (2.72)	4 (3.02)	3 (2.84)
Gender		3 (2.82)		4 (2.95)
Relationship duration	1 (2.11)	1 (1.38)	3 (2.88)	2 (2.16)
Relatedness to mother	3 (2.46)			5 (3.08)
Emotional insecurity with mother	4 (3.38)	6 (2.95)	1 (1.34)	1 (2.10)
Negative conflict with mother		5 (2.94)		
Emotional insecurity with father			2 (2.73)	6 (3.26)
Negative conflict with father		4 (2.83)		

Notes: Only above-threshold effects. Not shown due to the lack of predictive power: Effects of economic deprivation, school education, relatedness with father, compliance with mother/father, and maternal/paternal dominance.

Furthermore, emotional insecurity with mother was most important for emotional insecurity and autonomy in the romantic relationship. Beyond background factors, each romantic outcome (except for autonomy) was most strongly or exclusively linked to the same dimension of adolescents' relationships with both parents, suggesting higher salience of within-domain continuity than spill-over effects. However, clear domain-specific continuity was found for negative conflict only. In contrast, emotional insecurity with mother evidenced most global effects, as it spilled over into emotional insecurity, autonomy, relatedness, and negative conflict with partner. Overall, adolescents' relationship with mother proved more important (7 effects) than their relationship with father (3 effects).

LINEARITY OF EFFECTS AND INTERACTION EFFECTS

A closer inspection of links between predictor and outcome variables indicated weak non-linear effects of most predictors. Regarding *relatedness with partner* (see Figure 2), partnership duration contributed to a decrease within the second year of the partnership, which later levelled off. Age showed an inverted U-shape effect with increases in relatedness up to age 18.3 and a decrease thereafter. Relatedness with mother was positively linked to relatedness with partner, but not at its extremes (< 3 and > 4). The negative effect of emotional insecurity with mother was more pronounced in the lower range of emotional insecurity (< 3). A similar inverse pattern was found for the effects on *negative conflict with partner* (not shown). Negative conflict increased within the first 2 years only, and the effects of negative conflict with either parent were less

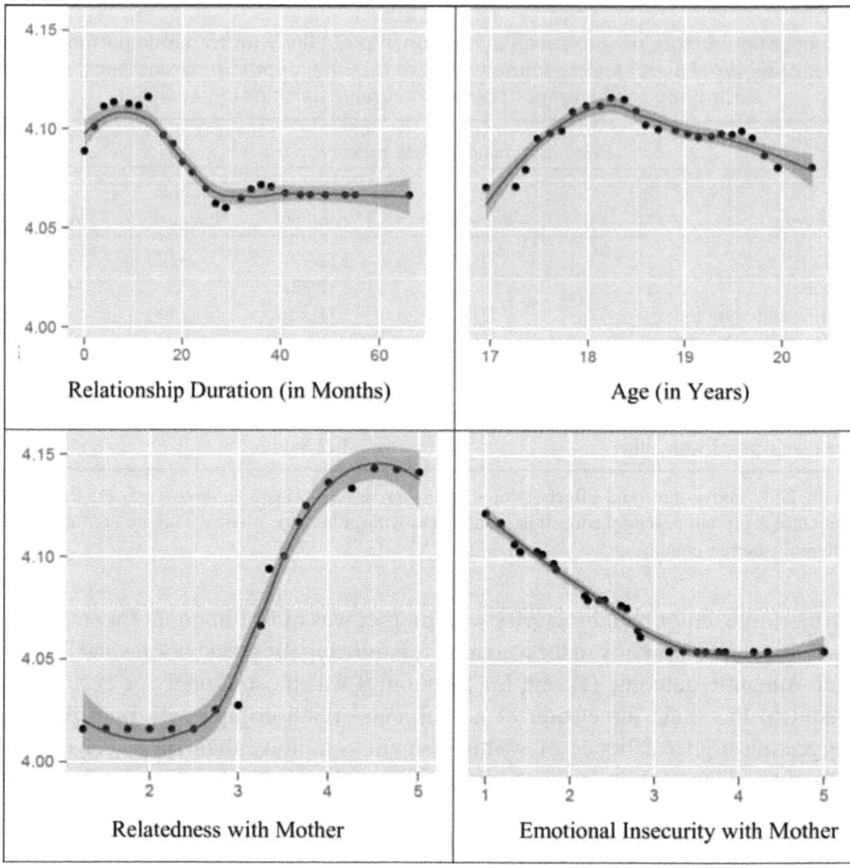

Figure 2. Effects of relationship duration, age, relatedness and emotional insecurity with mother on relatedness with romantic partner.

evident at the extremes of these indicators (< 2 and > 4). Emotional insecurity with mother was positively linked to negative conflict in the lower range of emotional insecurity (< 3), whereas further increases did not contribute to more conflict. Females reported more negative conflict than males.

Similar non-linear effects of emotional insecurity with parents were also found for *emotional insecurity with partner* (see Figure 3). Partnership duration evidenced a U-shaped link to emotional insecurity in the romantic relationship: emotional insecurity decreased during the first year and then increased up to 30 months, remaining below initial levels. In long-term relationships (2.5 years and more), however, emotional insecurity was no longer affected by relationship duration. The age effect was weak, with a slight decrease in emotional insecurity until age 17.7 years. Regarding *autonomy in the partnership*, differences by

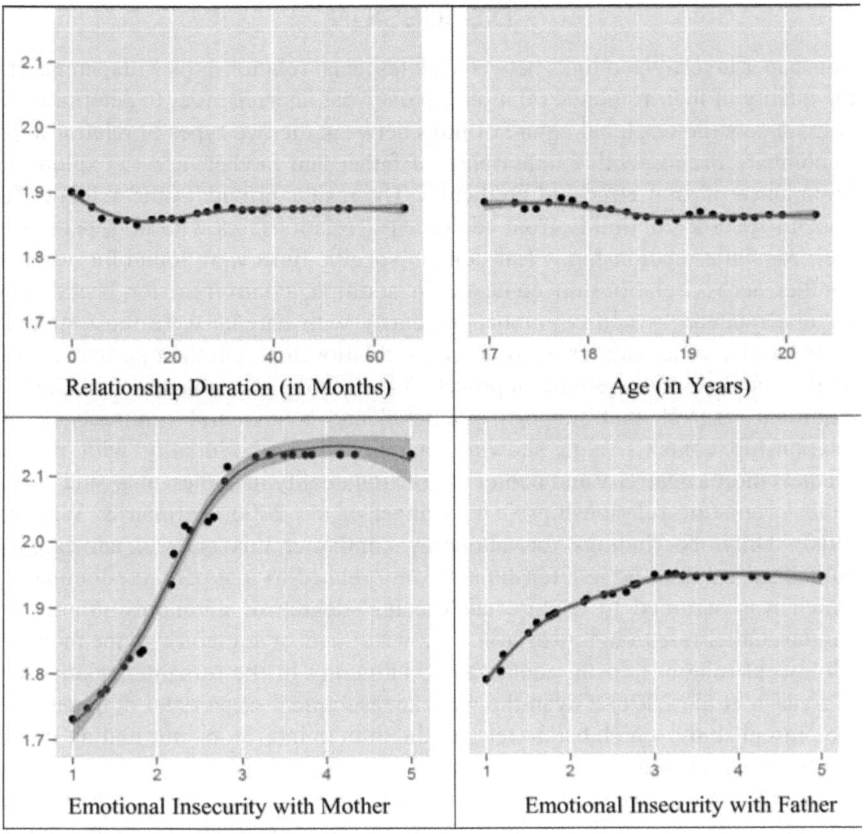

Figure 3. Effects of relationship duration, age and emotional insecurity with mother and father on emotional insecurity with romantic partner.

partnership duration emerged mostly in the first year, with those in shorter relationships reporting higher autonomy. With respect to age, a small decrease in autonomy was found after age 19 years. Females reported higher autonomy in their romantic relationships than males. Emotional insecurity with mother or father was inversely linked to autonomy with a non-linear trend. As before, both predictors had the strongest impact in the lower range of values with no additional effects at high levels of emotional insecurity (>3).

Further inspection of minimal depth for joint effects of predictors did not point to any substantial interaction effects. None of these effects reached a sufficiently low level of minimal depth. Hence, no evidence was found for the moderating role of relationship duration or contributions of specific predictor constellations, e.g., high relatedness combined with low emotional insecurity with parents, as one might expect from an attachment perspective.

DISCUSSION

This paper investigated links between adolescents' relationships with parents and the quality of their romantic relationship one year later, in order to determine the domain-specific or global nature of links between the two types of relationships, to compare the respective importance of father and mother, and to explore the importance of joint effects of predictors. The results provide some evidence for domain-specific continuity from adolescents' relationships with both parents to their romantic relationship. Clear domain-specific links were found for negative conflict across relationship contexts. In addition, controlling for background factors, relatedness and emotional insecurity with parents were most strongly linked to the same features of adolescents' relationship with their partner. In line with a behavioural systems approach, these findings resonate with existing empirical research that supports emotional and behavioural continuity across relationship contexts, e.g., showing that negative emotionality with parents predicts more negativity and poorer interaction quality in adolescents' and young adults' romantic relationships (e.g., Conger et al., 2000; Furman & Winkles, 2010). Only the findings for autonomy contradict this pattern: adolescents' autonomy in romantic relationships was not related to low parental dominance, which was assumed to capture adolescents' degree of autonomy granted by parents. Other research, however, has shown effects of autonomy in the mother–adolescent relationship on adolescents' autonomy in the romantic relationship (Taradash et al., 2001). Given the weak measurement of parental dominance in the present study, which had to rely on single-item indicators, our finding should not be overstretched.

In addition to these domain-specific links, we found evidence for the broader relevance of emotional insecurity with mother, as it proved important in predicting all four outcome variables. It not only undermined relatedness and triggered negative conflict but—in line with other evidence (e.g., Lavy, Mikulincer, & Shaver, 2010)—also interfered with autonomy in the romantic relationship. These findings render further support for attachment theory, which stresses the profound importance of secure attachment with primary caregivers for adolescents' later emotion regulation and their successful coping with interpersonal demands (Grossmann et al., 2002). Yet, contrary to the prominent role of typologies in attachment research (e.g., Bartholomew & Horowitz, 1991; Crowell, Fraley, & Shaver, 2008), our data did not identify relevant predictive power of specific constellations in adolescents' relationship with parents (e.g., marked by high relatedness and low emotional insecurity with parents).

In contrast, our expectations regarding global effects of relatedness were not fully supported by the data. Relatedness to mother seemed to facilitate relatedness and autonomy with partner, but neither prevented negative conflict nor emotional insecurity. Relatedness to father did not matter at all. Overall, our study adds to the evidence that mothers play a more important role than fathers in providing relationship experiences relevant for romantic development (e.g., Reese-Weber & Kahn, 2005; Seiffge-Krenke et al., 2010). The way how adolescents relate to their mother was more strongly and more consistently linked to their romantic relationship quality.

This study benefited from the large sample size and the longitudinal design. At the same time, it has limitations because it relies exclusively on adolescents' reports. Despite shortcomings of this mono-method approach, adolescents' appraisals are most important in predicting future behaviour (Grossmann et al., 2002). Furthermore, some bias should be attenuated by assessing adolescents' relationship with parents one year prior to the quality of romantic relationships.

Our findings have practical implications. In particular, they suggest addressing relationship experiences with parents when seeking to promote positive romantic development among young people. Although the effects reported here are small, emotional insecurity with parents seems to be a broadly relevant risk factor, which is likely to foreshadow partnership problems.

REFERENCES

Auslander, B. A., Short, M. B., Succop, P. A., & Rosenthal, S. L. (2009). Associations between parenting behaviors and adolescent romantic relationships. *Journal of Adolescent Health, 45*, 98–101. doi:10.1016/j.jadohealth.2008.12.014

Bartholomew, K., & Horowitz, L. M. (1991). Attachment styles among young adults: A test of a four-category model. *Journal of Personality and Social Psychology, 61*, 226–244. doi:10.1037/0022-3514.61.2.226

Bryant, C. M., & Conger, R. D. (2002). An intergenerational model of romantic relationship development. In A. L. Vangelisti, H. T. Reis, & M. A. Fitzpatrick (Eds.), *Stability and change in relationships* (pp. 57–82). New York, NY: Cambridge University Press.

Collins, N. L., & Feeney, B. C. (2000). A safe haven: An attachment theory perspective on support seeking and caregiving in intimate relationships. *Journal of Personality and Social Psychology, 78*, 1053–1073. doi:10.1037/0022-3514.78.6.1053

Collins, W. A., Welsh, D. P., & Furman, W. (2009). Adolescent romantic relationships. *Annual Review of Psychology, 60*, 631–652. doi:10.1146/annurev.psych.60.110707.163459

Conger, R. D., Cui, M., Bryant, C. M., & Elder, G. H. (2000). Competence in early adult romantic relationships: A developmental perspective on family influences. *Journal of Personality and Social Psychology, 79*, 224–237. doi:10.1037/0022-3514.79.2.224

Connolly, J., & Goldberg, A. (1999). Romantic relationships in adolescence. The role of friends and peers in their emergence and development. In W. Furman, B. B. Brown & C. Feiring (Eds.), *The development of romatic relationships in adolescence* (pp. 266–290). Cambridge: University Press.

Crockett, L. J., & Randall, B. A. (2006). Linking adolescent family and peer relationships to the quality of young adult romantic relationships: The mediating role of conflict tactics. *Journal of Social and Personal Relationships, 23*, 761–780. doi:10.1177/0265407506068262

Crowell, J. A., Fraley, R. C., & Shaver, P. R. (2008). Measurement of individual differences in adolescent and adult attachment. In J. Cassidy & P. R. Shaver (Eds.), *Handbook of attachment: Theory, research, and clinical applications* (2nd ed., pp. 599–634). New York, NY: Guilford Press.

Darling, N., Cohan, C. L., Burns, A., & Thompson, L. (2008). Within-family conflict behaviors as predictors of conflict in adolescent romantic relations. *Journal of Adolescence, 31*, 671–690. doi:10.1016/j.adolescence.2008.10.003

Doyle, A. B., Lawford, H., & Markiewicz, D. (2009). Attachment style with mother, father, best friend, and romantic partner during adolescence. *Journal of Research on Adolescence, 19*, 690–714. doi:10.1111/j.1532-7795.2009.00617.x

Duemmler, S. L., & Kobak, R. (2001). The development of commitment and attachment in dating relationships: Attachment security as relationship construct. *Journal of Adolescence, 24*, 401–415. doi:10.1006/jado.2001.0406

Furman, W., & Buhrmester, D. (1985). Children's perceptions of the personal relationships in their social networks. *Developmental Psychology, 21*, 1016–1024. doi:10.1037/0012-1649.21.6.1016

Furman, W., & Wehner, E. A. (1994). Romantic views: Toward a theory of adolescent romantic relationships. In R. Montemayor, G. R. Adams, & T. P. Gullotta (Eds.), *Personal relationships during adolescence* (pp. 168–195). Thousand Oaks, CA: Sage Publications.

Furman, W., & Wehner, E. (1997). Adolescent romantic relationships: A developmental perspective. In S. Shulman & A. W. Collins (Eds.), *New directions for child development, Number 78: Adolescent romantic relationships* (pp. 21–36). San Francisco, CA: Jossey-Bass.

Furman, W., & Winkles, J. K. (2010). Predicting romantic involvement, relationship cognitions, and relationship qualities from physical appearance, perceived norms, and relational styles regarding friends and parents. *Journal of Adolescence, 33*, 827–836. doi:10.1016/j.adolescence.2010.07.004

Grossmann, K. E., Grossmann, K., Winter, M., & Zimmermann, P. (2002). Attachment relationships and appraisal of partnership: From early experience of sensitive support to later relationship representation. In L. Pulkkinen & A. Caspi (Eds.), *Paths to successful development* (pp. 73–105). Cambridge, MA: Cambridge University Press.

Grusec, J. E., & Davidov, M. (2010). Integrating different perspectives on socialization theory and research: A domain-specific approach. *Child Development, 81*, 687–709. doi:10.1111/j.1467-8624.2010.01426.x

Hare, A. L., Miga, E. M., & Allen, J. P. (2009). Intergenerational transmission of aggression in romantic relationships: The moderating role of attachment security. *Journal of Family Psychology, 23*, 808–818. doi:10.1037/a0016740

Huinink, J., Brüderl, J., Nauck, B., Walper, S., Castiglioni, L., & Feldhaus, M. (2011). Panel analysis of intimate relationships and family dynamics (pairfam): Conceptual framework and design. *Zeitschrift für Familienforschung/Journal of Family Research, 23*, 77–101. doi:10.4232/pairfam.5678.5.0.0

Kruse, J., & Walper, S. (2008). Types of individuation in relation to parents: Predictors and outcomes. *International Journal of Behavioural Development, 32*, 390–400. doi:10.1177/0165025408093657

Lavy, S., Mikulincer, M., & Shaver, P. R. (2010). Autonomy-proximity imbalance: An attachment theory perspective on intrusiveness in romantic relationships. *Personality and Individual Differences, 48*, 552–556. doi:10.1016/j.paid.2009.12.004

McClanahan, G., & Holmbeck, G. N. (1992). Separation-individuation, family functioning, and psychological adjustment in college students: A construct validity study of the separation-individuation test of adolescence. *Journal of Personality Assessment, 59*, 468–485. doi:10.1207/s15327752jpa5903_4

Merkle, E. C., & Shaffer, V. A. (2011). Binary recursive partitioning: Background, methods, and application to psychology. *British Journal of Mathematical and Statistical Psychology, 64*, 161–181. doi:10.1348/000711010X503129

Olson, D. H., McCubbin, H. I., Barnes, H., Larson, A., Muxen, M. J., & Wilson, M. A. (1983). *Families. What makes them work*. Newbury Park: Sage.

Pascuzzo, K., Cyr, C., & Moss, E. (2013). Longitudinal association between adolescent attachment, adult romantic attachment, and emotion regulation strategies. *Attachment & Human Development, 15*, 83–103. doi:10.1080/14616734.2013.745713

R Core Team. (2015). R: A language and environment for statistical computing. Reference Index. Version 3.1.3. Retrieved from http://cran.r-project.org/doc/manuals/r-release/fullrefman.pdf

Reese-Weber, M., & Kahn, J. H. (2005). Familial predictors of sibling and romantic-partner conflict resolution: Comparing late adolescents from intact and divorced families. *Journal of Adolescence, 28*, 479–493. doi:10.1016/j.adolescence.2004.09.004

Roisman, G., Collins, W. A., Sroufe, L. A., & Egeland, B. (2005). Predictors of young adults' representations of and behavior in their current romantic relationship: Prospective tests of the prototype hypothesis. *Attachment and Human Development, 7*, 105–121. doi:10.1080/14616730500134928

Saraiva, L. M., & Matos, P. M. (2012). Separation-individuation of Portuguese emerging adults in relation to parents and to the romantic partner. *Journal of Youth Studies, 15*, 499–517. doi:10.1080/13676261.2012.663889

Scharf, M., & Mayseless, O. (2008). Late adolescent girls' relationships with parents and romantic partner: The distinct role of mothers and fathers. *Journal of Adolescence, 31*, 837–855. doi:10.1016/j.adolescence.2008.06.012

Schneewind, K. A., & Kruse, J. (Eds.). (2002). *Die Paarklimaskalen (PKS)* [The partnership climate scales]. Bern: Verlag Hans Huber.

Seiffge-Krenke, I. (2003). Testing theories of romantic development from adolescence to young adulthood: Evidence of a developmental sequence. *International Journal of Behavioral Development, 27*, 519–531. doi:10.1080/01650250344000145

Seiffge-Krenke, I., Overbeek, G., & Vermulst, A. (2010). Parent–child relationship trajectories during adolescence: Longitudinal associations with romantic outcomes in emerging adulthood. *Journal of Adolescence, 33*, 159–171. doi:10.1016/j.adolescence.2009.04.001

Strobl, C., Malley, J., & Tutz, G. (2009). An introduction to recursive partitioning: Rationale, application, and characteristics of classification and regression trees, bagging, and random forests. *Psychological Methods, 14*, 323–348. doi:10.1037/a0016973

Taradash, A., Connolly, J., Pepler, D., Craig, W., & Costa, M. (2001). The interpersonal context of romantic autonomy in adolescence. *Journal of Adolescence, 24*, 365–377. doi:10.1006/jado.2001.0404

Thönnissen, C., Gschwendtner, C., Wilhelm, B., Fiedrich, S., Wendt, E.-V., & Walper, S. (2014). Scales Manual of the German Family Panel. Waves 1 to 5. Release 5.0. Revised since Release 4.0, May 2013. With contributions from: Petra Buhr, Veronika Salzburger, Nadia Lois, & Claudia Schmiedeberg. pairfam Panel Analysis of Intimate Relationships and Family Dynamics. Retrieved from http://www.pairfam.de/fileadmin/user_upload/redakteur/publis/Dokumentation/Manuals/Scales_Manual_pairfam_5.0.pdf

Walper, S. (2009). Links of perceived economic deprivation to adolescents' well-being six years later. *Zeitschrift für Familienforschung/Journal of Family Research, 21*, 107–127. Retrieved from http://www.zeitschrift-fuer-familienforschung.de/pdf/2009-2-walper.pdf

Youniss, J., & Smollar, J. (1985). *Adolescent relations with mothers, fathers, and friends*. Chicago, IL: The University of Chicago Press.

APPENDIX

TABLE A1
Correlations of indicators of relationship quality with mother, father (t2), and romantic partner (t3).

	1	*2*	*3*	*4*	*5*	*6*	*7*	*8*	*9*	*10*	*11*	*12*	*13*	*14*
1. Relatedness w. M	1													
2. Relatedness w. F	.64***	1												
3. Emotional insecurity w. M	−.27***	−.23***	1											
4. Emotional insecurity w. F	−.20***	−.35***	.72***	1										
5. Neg. conflict w. M	−.39***	−.24***	.25***	.20***	1									
6. Neg. conflict w. F	−.17***	−.41***	.20***	.35***	.41***	1								
7. Dominance M	.04	.05	.17***	.12**	.17***	.10**	1							
8. Dominance F	.08*	.11**	.07*	.08*	.02	.10**	.66***	1						
9. Compliance w. M	.06	.10*	.05	−.05	.16***	−.04	.19***	.07	1					
10. Compliance w. F	.05	.01	.01	.07	.03	.17***	.14***	.26***	.37***	1				
11. Relatedness w. P	.18***	.17***	−.14***	−.11**	−.08*	−.12**	.03	−.05	.00	−.02	1			
12. Emotional insecurity w. P	−.10**	−.10*	.31***	.25***	.13**	.13***	.03	−.01	.04	.05	−.28***	1		
13. Neg. conflict w. P	−.04	−.09*	.19***	.19***	.19***	.19***	.04	.03	.00	−.00	−.25***	.29***	1	
14. Autonomy w. P	.15***	.14***	−.19***	−.14***	−.10*	−.08*	−.08*	−.07	.02	.00	.27***	−.16***	−.34***	1
15. Partnership duration	.07	.08*	−.08*	−.08*	−.05	−.12**	−.04	−.02	−.10**	−.06	−.05	−.02	.19***	−.07

Note: N: 694–719; M = Mother; F = Father; P = Partner. Significance: $*p < .05$. $**p < .01$. $***p < .001$.

Gendered pathways to romantic attachment in emerging adults: The role of body image and parental support

Inge Seiffge-Krenke[1], Malte Persike[1], and Shmuel Shulman[2]

[1]Department of Psychology, Mainz University, Mainz, Germany
[2]Department of Psychology, Bar Ilan University, Ramat Gan, Israel

This study analyses the impact of body image and perceived parental behaviour (support and negativity) as factors that contribute to romantic attachment in emerging adulthood. In a 11-year longitudinal study on 144 females and 114 males, we assessed body image, body mass index, and perceived father's and mother's support and negativity during adolescence (at ages 14 and 17) and in emerging adulthood (age 21). At the age of 25, romantic attachment was assessed. Results of path analyses revealed that females' positive body image was consistently linked with greater parental support over time and contributed to low avoidance in romance at the age of 25, whereas perceived negativity with fathers mediated by body image contributed to more avoidance in females' later romantic relationships. In contrast, parental support and negativity during adolescence and young adulthood had no impact; only a positive body image resulted in males' low avoidance in later romantic attachment at the age of 25. The findings point to gendered socialization for males and females and highlight the importance of body image for an adaptive romantic outcome in emerging adulthood.

During pubertal development, adolescents begin to experience longing for sexual gratification and emotional closeness with a partner, but only after consolidation of their body image adolescents are capable of adaptively seeking a potential partner (Laufer & Laufer, 1984). Subsequently, adolescents learn to interact with the other gender and learn how to relate competently to a romantic partner (Brown, 1999; Connolly & McIsaac, 2009). During this developmental process,

No potential conflict of interest was reported by the authors.

supportive relationships with parents were associated with more secure relational styles in later romantic relationships (Furman & Shomaker, 2008; Hazan & Shaver, 1987). Through the acceptance of one's changing body and emerging sexuality combined with supportive experiences in close relationships (ECRs), adolescents learn to become engaged and invested in romantic relationships (Furman & Wehner, 1997). The purpose of the current study was to examine the extent to which the developmental courses of body image and parental support through adolescence can explain the quality of heterosexual romantic attachment during emerging adulthood.

Body Image in Romantic Encounters: A Neglected Perspective

A large body of research has demonstrated the contribution of earlier experiences with parents to romantic development (for a summary, see Collins, Welsh, & Furman, 2009; Seiffge-Krenke & Shulman, 2012). However, few studies have examined the importance of the maturing body (Seiffge-Krenke, Shulman, & Kiessinger, 2001) or investigated how sexuality is integrated and develops within the framework of adolescent romantic relationships (Shulman, Walsh, Weisman, & Schelyer, 2009).

Our research aimed to explore the role of body image during adolescence as a precursor of romantic attachment in emerging adulthood. As a part of the self-concept, body image involves subjective evaluations of the body. These include affective, cognitive and behavioural components and are related to various aspects such as body size, attractiveness, physical functioning, fitness and health (Davison & McCabe, 2006). During adolescence, body image accommodates physical changes. Adolescents' changing physical appearance, their increasing cognitive abilities and the social comparison with peers typically foster a heightened awareness of or preoccupation with their own and others' perceptions of their bodies (Compian, Gowen, & Hayward, 2004).

To be able to establish romantic relationships, adolescents must adapt to their changing bodies (Laufer & Laufer, 1984). Romantic interactions and relationships are new experiences for adolescents. In addition, adolescents need to become aware of their sexuality and sexual attraction and learn adaptive ways to express these emerging wishes and fantasies. After adolescents accumulate experience with transient romantic and sexual encounters and their body image has matured, they are capable to establish meaningful romantic relationships. Research has not directly answered whether a positive body image facilitates romantic involvement and contributes to later romantic attachment. However, some studies have focused on the importance of physical changes, dieting behaviour, and attractiveness for romantic involvement and quality. Early maturing adolescents (Collins et al., 2009) as well as those who perceive themselves as attractive (Simon, Aikins, & Prinstein, 2008) start to date earlier and become more seriously involved in dating. Furthermore, attractiveness has been found to be related to more romantic satisfaction (Furman & Winkles, 2010). Adolescent females who date are more likely to be dieting (Compian et al., 2004). A higher body mass index (BMI) is associated with a lower likelihood of dating in male and female adolescents (Halpern, King, Oslak, & Udry, 2005), and young people during emerging adulthood reporting greater bodily esteem were more likely to be romantically involved. However, the research has not investigated the longitudinal effects of a more positive body image during adolescence on the quality of romantic attachment during emerging adulthood.

Relationships with Parents: The Distinct Roles of Mothers and Fathers

Parent–child relationships have been conceived as the central context in which children learn how to form and maintain a romantic relationship (Seiffge-Krenke & Shulman, 2012). Experiencing closeness, support and trust with parents is internalized and carried forward into later romantic relationships (Furman, Simon, Shaffer, & Bouchey, 2002; Seiffge-Krenke et al., 2001). In this study, we focused on two central dimensions of parent–child relationships, namely, perceived support and negativity. Support relates to a sense of interpersonal warmth, closeness and understanding; negativity relates to negative affect, conflicts and unconstructive negotiation. Overall, supportive parent–child relationships are associated with stable, positive romantic relationships in adolescence and emerging adulthood (Collins & Van Dulmen, 2006). Late adolescents who report supportive relationships with their parents also report closer and more secure relational styles in their romantic relationships (Furman & Shomaker, 2008). Supportive relationships with parents were associated with adolescents' romantic quality (Engels, Finkenauer, Meeus, & Dekovic, 2001), whereas negative emotionality (e.g., anger, ambivalence) in parent–adolescent dyads was predictive of poor quality interactions with romantic partners in late adolescence (Kim & Capaldi, 2004).

The children's relationship with the mother differs from that with the father in quality and potential implications for body image and romantic attachment (Dalton III, Frick-Horbury, & Kitzmann, 2006) Studies have demonstrated that the relationships with mothers are closer, but that they also involve higher levels of conflict than those with fathers (Scharf & Mayseless, 2008; Seiffge-Krenke, Overbeek, & Vermulst, 2010). Furthermore, the mother–daughter dyad is much closer than all other dyads in the family (Mayseless, Wiseman, & Hai, 1998). Research has shown that, in general, boys learn from their mothers and girls from their fathers how to behave in heterosexual romantic relationships (Bucx & Seiffge-Krenke, 2010; Feldman, Gowen, & Fisher, 1998). Girls also seem to learn feminine behaviours by complementing their fathers' masculine behaviours (Shulman & Seiffge-Krenke, 1997).

Gray and Steinberg (1999) proposed that the quality of relationships with parents is also linked with the development of an adaptive body image and sexual interests. Developmentally, appropriate parental support may be helpful during adolescence when coping with one's maturing body (Laufer & Laufer, 1984). Respectful and more general support seem to be most appropriate because the adolescent is more likely to feel comfortable and accepted (Snary, 1993). Alternatively, negativity in parent–child relationships could be detrimental for the child's body image. So far, research has focused on parents' direct and controlling comments regarding appearance and weight, particularly in daughters (Cromley, Neumark-Sztainer, Story, & Boutelle, 2010; Stice & Whitenton, 2002), and their negative impact on body image. The extent that parents contribute to a positive body image via general and respectful support, however, needs to be explored. Given the proposed centrality of body image in romantic relationships, the link between parental support and an adaptive body concept should be examined, particularly how the developmental course of these two variables during adolescence explains the quality of romantic attachment in emerging adulthood. Finally, the consideration of the possible distinctive maternal and paternal roles in adolescent development warrants analysis of whether maternal and paternal support will associate differently with the consolidation of an adaptive body image and subsequent romantic attachment.

The Present Study

In a 11-year longitudinal study, we explored the links between support/negativity in parent–child relationships as perceived by participants when they were 14, 17 and 21 years old and romantic attachment to a heterosexual partner at the age of 25. Body image was assessed two times during adolescence, at the age of 14 when participants are in the process of physical maturity and at the age of 17, when their body has reached its more mature form. These ages are also crucial with respect to romantic involvement, as most romantic relationships are initiated around the age of 14, whereas around the age of 17 dyadic relationships are formed, and eventually more stable relationships develop (Seiffge-Krenke & Shulman, 2012). We measured romantic attachment at the age of 25 when the participants were expected to be in more enduring, intimate and romantic relationships. We controlled for BMI, because it is closely linked to feelings of attractiveness (Rosenblum & Lewis, 1999), dieting behaviour and romantic involvement (Compian et al., 2004).

METHOD

Participants

The participants of this study ($N = 258$, 144 females) were part of a longitudinal sample of families whose adolescent children had been followed until the age of

25. The study received institutional review board approval from the first author's home university. The participants' mean age was 14.27 years (SD = 1.41) at the beginning of the study. All of the participants' parents provided informed consent at the beginning of the study and at the second assessment (mean age 16.95, SD = 1.4). At two later time points, the emerging adult participants (mean age 21.3, SD = 1.4 and 25. 2, SD = 1.2) provided written consent. Most of the participants (94%) were German and came from families with two biological parents (85%); 15% were raised in single-mother families. The overall sample was representative of German society (Statistisches Bundesamt, 2013) with respect to socioeconomic backgrounds (15% of the families having high, 52% middle and 23% low SES), family size (mean number of siblings = 1.39, SD = 1.22) and parents' employment status (79% of the fathers and 58% of the mothers were employed full-time, and 6% of the fathers and 8% of the mothers were unemployed).

At the age of 25, 77% reported having a romantic partner. At this age, 33% of the participants were still residing with their parents, 18% lived with a partner, and the others either lived alone (27%) or in shared apartments (22%), which is typical for young adult Germans (Seiffe-Krenke, 2006). Sixty-four per cent of the participants had a high level of secondary schooling (i.e., had completed 13 years of high school and received the *Abitur*, a requirement for admittance to German universities). At the age of 25, 57% of the participants were enrolled in higher educational or vocational programmes (40% studying, 17% in apprenticeships), 37% were employed and 6% were unemployed.

Instruments

Attachment to partner. At the age of 25, participants completed the ECRs survey (Brennan, Clark, & Shaver, 1998), which consists of 36 items ranked on a scale ranging from 1 (*strongly disagree*) to 7 (*strongly agree*). In this study, the subscale *anxiety* (18 items) described the extent to which participants were insecure about their partner's availability and responsiveness. The subscale *avoidance* (18 items) described the extent to which participants were uncomfortable about being close to and dependent upon their partner. Internal consistencies for anxiety were .83; internal consistencies for avoidance were .81.

Perceived parental social support and negativity. At ages 14, 17 and 21, participants completed the Network of Relationships Inventory (Furman & Buhrmester, 1985), responding to items that assessed maternal and paternal social support (the same items were used for each relationship). Seven of the original 10 subscales were used for *social support* (companionship, instrumental aid, satisfaction, nurturance, affection, admiration and reliable alliance; each with three items). Punishment and conflict (each with three items) were used to assess *negativity*. Participants rated the items on a scale ranging from 1 (*little or none*) to 5 (*the most*). Means were computed for each subscale, creating separate scores for each relationship for each time of measurement. Internal reliability was high for perceived maternal social support ($\alpha = .80$ to. 82) and for perceived paternal social support ($\alpha = .82$ to .84), as well as for fathers' negativity ($\alpha = .78$ to .83) and mothers' negativity ($\alpha = .80$ to .85).

Adolescent body image. At ages 14 and 17, participants completed the Frankfurter Scales of Body Concept (FKKS; Deusinger, 1998). The FKKS is a 36-item questionnaire that measures body image belonging to three subscales: body strength/competence, body attractiveness and body feelings. Items were rated on each scale ranging from 1 (*strongly disagree*) to 5 (*strongly agree*). In the present study, item scores were summed across subscales. Internal reliability of the total score was good ($\alpha = .83$ to .86).

Body mass index. Based on the participants' reported heights and weights at ages 14 and 25, a BMI for each participant was calculated (BMI = kg/m^2).

Plan of Analyses

Missing data accounted for an average of 4.13% of reports for the variables included in this study (range = .0–11.5%). No statistically significant differences on any demographic, control or study variables were found between those who participated at all time points and those who did not. However, Little's test indicated that data were not missing at random (MNAR), $\chi^2(112) = 365.3$, $p < .001$. For path analyses, missing data were completed by multiple imputation.

Preliminary analyses examined gender differences for potential covariates such as BMI and the main study variables (parental support, parental negativity, body image and romantic attachment). Path analyses were then conducted to predict two facets of romantic attachment (avoidance and anxiety) at the age of 25 from parental support and negativity at younger ages from 14 to 21, mediated by body image. Path models were tested in a structural equation modelling framework with Mplus (Muthén & Muthén, 2010). The multiple group mediation design, with gender as the grouping factor, accounted for differences between male and female participants in unique associations between the predictor variables, parental support and negativity, and the outcome variable, romantic attachment, mediated by body image. Path analyses for the reported study variables were conducted separately with respect to mothers and fathers. In both analyses, parental support and negativity at ages 14, 17 and 21 were predictor variables, romantic attachment (avoidance and anxiety at the age of 25) was the outcome variable, and body image at ages 14 and 17 were mediator variables.

BMI as a potential covariate was partialed out of body image and outcome variables before path analyses by computing a simple regression and only entering the residuals into the model. Model fit was assessed on the basis of a combined evaluation of multiple fit indices. Fit was considered good, with root mean square error of approximation (RMSEA) $< .08$, comparative fit index (CFI) $> .95$, Tucker-Lewis Index (TLI) $> .95$, and standardized root mean squared residual (SRMR) $< .05$ (Hu & Bentler, 1999). Significant differences between male and female participants in the indirect association from parental support and negativity to romantic attachment via body image was detected using Wald χ^2 tests with $df = 1$.

RESULTS

Table 1 presents means, standard deviations and correlations for BMI as well as the study variables perceived parental support, negativity, adolescent body image and emerging adults' romantic attachment. Overall, romantic attachment at the age of 25 is good as shown by low avoidance and anxiety scores, and perceived maternal and paternal support are substantially higher than parental negativity at all ages. A series of Welch tests revealed no significant differences between female and male participants with respect to all measures.

TABLE 1
Descriptive statistics of the study variables

	Age (years)	*Female* M *(SD)*	*Male* M *(SD)*	*Total* M *(SD)*	N *Total (female)*	*Range Min, Max*
BMI	14	20.4 (2.8)	20.8 (5.0)	20.6 (3.9)	258 (144)	14.9, 36.9
	17	21.9 (2.6)	22.5 (2.7)	22.1 (2.7)	258 (144)	17.6, 30.7
	25	23.9 (2.2)	24.2 (3.2)	24.0 (2.7)	258 (144)	19.2, 33.5
Body image	14*	115.3 (14.9)	119.6 (17.7)	117.2 (16.3)	256 (144)	65, 155
	17	117.7 (15.5)	119.8 (17.6)	118.6 (16.5)	248 (140)	76, 147
Social support (mother)	14	72.5 (16.6)	73.4 (13.1)	72.9 (15.1)	248 (138)	28, 101
	17	72.0 (18.3)	72.2 (14.0)	72.1 (16.4)	240 (132)	28, 104
	21	74.0 (17.1)	69.6 (14.2)	72.0 (16.0)	258 (144)	22, 103
Negativity (mother)	14	13.2 (3.8)	13.4 (4.6)	13.3 (4.2)	248 (138)	6, 30
	17	13.1 (4.5)	13.0 (4.4)	13.1 (4.5)	240 (132)	6, 29
	21	12.1 (4.7)	12.1 (3.9)	12.1 (4.4)	258 (144)	1, 28
Social support (father)	14	63.7 (19.4)	67.4 (16.0)	65.3 (18.0)	236 (134)	5, 108
	17	66.2 (18.9)	67.0 (17.5)	66.6 (18.3)	228 (124)	21, 102
	21	65.8 (20.3)	68.3 (14.5)	66.9 (17.9)	258 (144)	21, 99
Negativity (father)	14	12.8 (4.6)	13.2 (4.5)	13.0 (4.5)	236 (134)	6, 27
	17	12.1 (3.9)	12.3 (3.6)	12.2 (3.8)	228 (124)	6, 25
	21	11.8 (4.5)	11.5 (3.4)	11.7 (4.0)	258 (144)	5, 30
Avoidance	25	2.3 (.9)	2.3 (1.0)	2.3 (.9)	258 (144)	.12, 4.47
Anxiety	25	2.9 (1.3)	3.2 (1.1)	3.0 (1.2)	258 (144)	.0, 6.52

Note: Significant differences between females and males are marked (*$p < .05$).

Path Models

Path coefficients in all models are standardized with respect to the variances of the continuous latent variables. The path model for interactions with mothers and their impact on later romantic attachment is depicted in Figure 1. Model fit was good (RMSEA = .067, CFI = .981, TLI = .951, SRMR = .042). Strong direct relations were found for males and females over time between perceived social support provided by mothers and between negativity in maternal interactions. Neither social support nor negativity, however, had any direct predictive power for later romantic attachment. For females, the indirect path from social support provided by

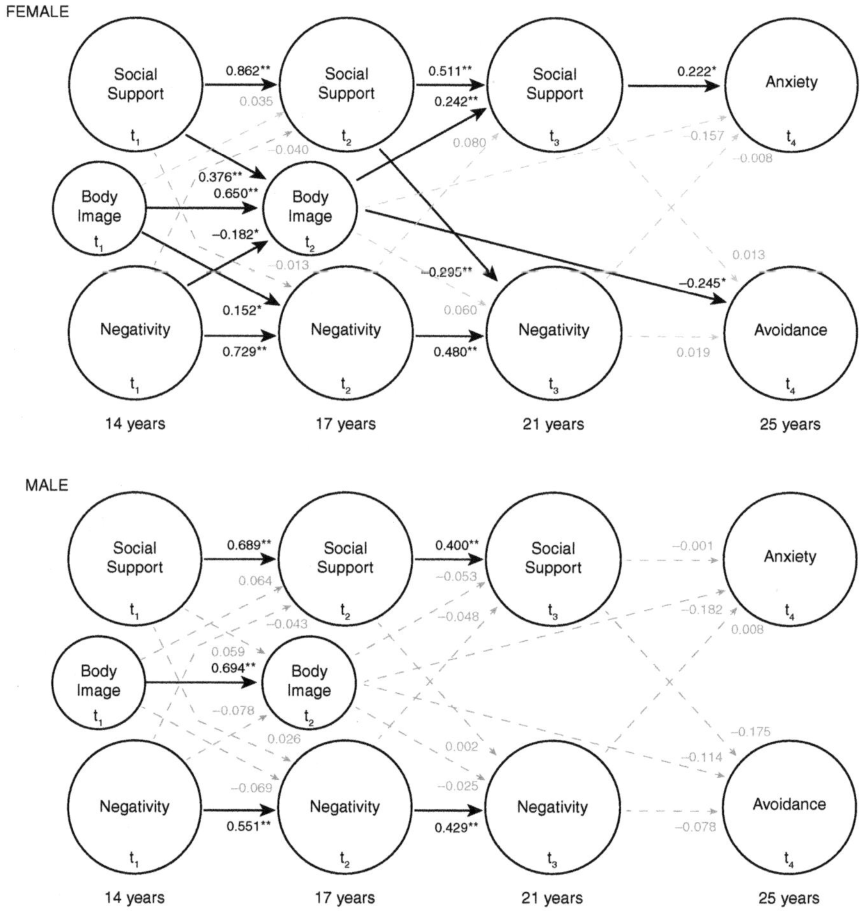

Figure 1. Structural model for maternal support and negativity. *Note:* Significance of path coefficients was computed against an expected value of zero (*$p < .05$, **$p < .01$). Insignificant paths are depicted in light grey. Indirect paths are not shown but discussed in the text. Within-time correlations between predictors and outcome variables are also not shown.

mothers to avoidant attachment in romantic relationships was mediated by body image ($\beta = -.053, p < .05$). Higher maternal support at early ages was correlated with a more positive body image in daughters, which in turn reduced avoidance in later romantic attachment. This indirect path was not found for males. Although a direct link between body image at early ages and avoidant attachment in romantic relationships at the age of 25 was found for males, body image did not function as a mediator for either social support provided by or negativity experienced with mothers. The prediction of avoidance by body image was comparable as strong, indicated by a non-significant Wald test ($p = .192$). No links between any predictor variable and anxiety in romantic relationships were found.

The path model for father interactions and their impact on later romantic attachment is summarized in Figure 2. Model fit was good (RMSEA = .032,

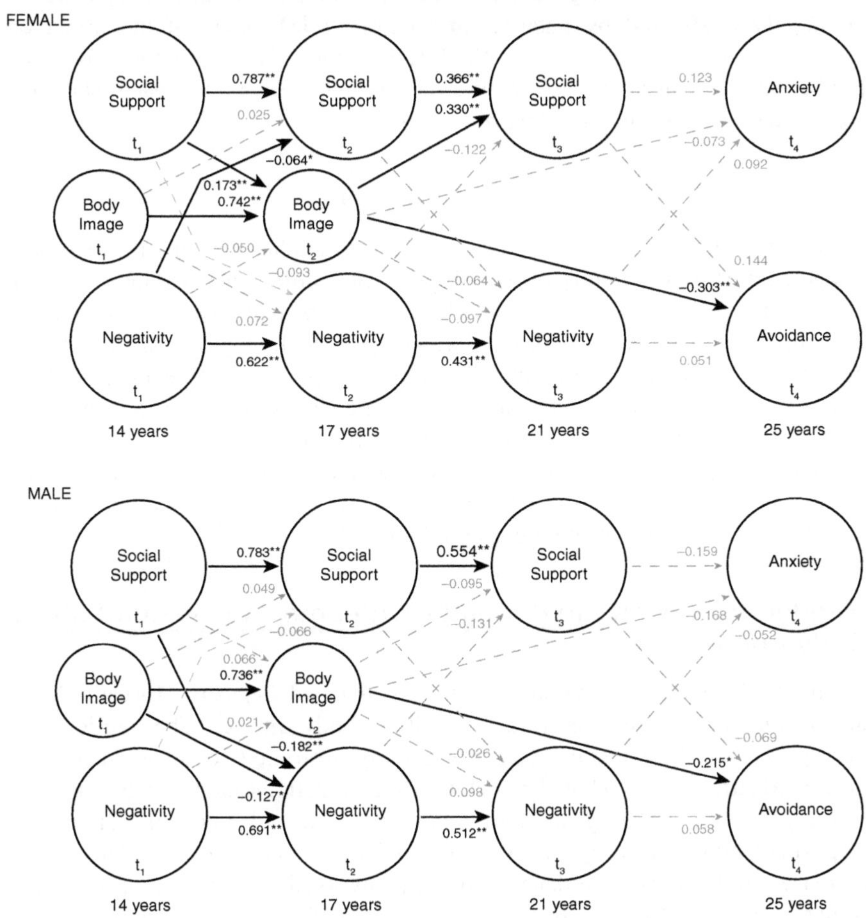

Figure 2. Structural model for paternal support and negativity. *Note:* Conventions as in Figure 1.

CFI = .995, TLI = .987, SRMR = .032). Similar to the results on maternal interactions, a strong direct connection between social support and negativity by fathers over time was found for both males and females. The pattern of associations, however, was more complex than for the maternal model. Body image of females was influenced by paternal social support and even more strongly by paternal negativity. Body image served as a predictor of avoidant attachment in later romantic relationships, but anxiety was only predicted by perceived paternal social support. The same indirect path from parental social support to avoidant attachment was found for females, mediated by body image ($\beta = -.092$, $p < .01$). Other than for interactions with mothers, daughters also showed an indirect path from negative paternal interactions to avoidant attachment, mediated by body image ($\beta = .044$, $p < .05$). No further indirect paths reached statistical significance. Romantic attachment of sons appeared to be largely unaffected by paternal interaction styles. None of the predictors reached statistical significance. Wald tests conducted to compare outcome prediction estimates between males and females failed to reach statistical significance (for all direct paths, $p > .146$).

DISCUSSION

This 11-year longitudinal study is one of the first studies that link positive body image with perceived family relationships during adolescence and later romantic attachment. At emerging adulthood, the majority of participants in our sample were involved in steady romantic relationships, which they described as low in anxiety and avoidance. Both females and males reporting a more adequate body image at the age of 17 described lower avoidance in the romantic relationships 8 years later. The findings shed light on the mechanisms by which fathers' and mothers' support or negativity influences later romantic attachment and highlights the central role of body image in shaping the quality of heterosexual romantic attachment during emerging adulthood.

Gendered Pathways to Romantic Outcome and the Centrality of Body Image

Similar to the findings of Wood-Barcalow, Tylka, and Augustus-Horvath (2010), all of our participants showed a positive body image. The participants' perceptions of their bodies were not merely restricted to appearance (e.g., perceived attractiveness) but also included body functions and feelings (Abbott & Barber, 2010), suggesting that participants generally felt good in their bodies. A positive body image by the time pubertal development is completed likely increases adolescents' confidence to become involved in more serious and stable romantic relationships (Kelly, Wall, Eisenberg, Story, & Neumark-Sztainer, 2005; Seiffge-Krenke, 2003; Shulman & Scharf, 2000). This statement can explain why body image at the age of 17 explained a more adaptive romantic attachment for both females and males (low avoidance and low anxiety) at emerging adulthood (i.e., 8 years later). Although we expected body image to serve as a precursor for an adaptive romantic outcome at the age of 25, we were astounded to see such a strong, consistent, long-term impact of body image on adaptive romantic attachment for both males and females.

Parental support was found to enhance adolescent body image (though only for females) which in turn affected romantic relationships after 8 years. This echoes existing research. Earlier studies reported that parental support serves as a buffer against body dissatisfaction and disturbed eating behaviours, which is frequently observed in adolescent females (Stice & Whitenton, 2002). Consequently, females in our study who developed a positive body image with the support of their parents during their adolescent years felt comfortable in being close to their romantic partners at the age of 25.

Previous research has focused on parents' comments about their daughter's body and the pressure to be thin (Stice & Whitenton, 2002), the encouragement to lose weight (McCabe & Ricciardelli, 2005; Murray, Byrne, & Rieger, 2011), and the modelling of negative eating attitudes and behaviours by the same-sex parent (Cromley et al., 2010). This type of parental influence has been reported to result in females' lower satisfaction with and more concern about their body (Blodgett Salafia & Gondoli, 2011; Cromley et al., 2010; Helfert & Warschburger, 2011). Our study showed that mothers and fathers can be influential in promoting their daughter's positive body image with support. The general support, which excluded teasing and comments about their daughter's physical appearance, was clearly helpful for establishing a positive body image, which led to more adaptive romantic relationships. However, negativity in father–daughter relationships also impacted body image, which in turn contributed to the daughters' higher avoidance in romantic attachment at the age of 25. This finding underscores that the opposite gender parent is also important for the formation of gender roles and body image (Bucx & Seiffge-Krenke, 2010) and that females are much more sensitive to their father's unsympathetic and non-supportive parenting behaviour than males.

Earlier research has shown that fathers and mothers react differently regarding their sons' and daughters' romantic involvement. Kan, McHale, and Crouter (2008) demonstrated that fathers permit more autonomy in their sons but are more restrictive towards their daughters' involvement in romantic relationships. Madsen (2008) found that parents regulate their daughters' dating activities more often than their sons'. Rule sets for daughters are more likely to include adult supervision so that parents can maintain a greater degree of control over their daughters' dating activities (e.g., rules about curfews, rules about when, how much and whom a daughter dates).

Our findings showed a differential gender-related impact of support and negativity on children's body image and later romantic outcomes. Paternal negativity affected daughters' but not sons' body image. Paternal support combined with paternal strictness and supervision can possibly foster a girl's ability to learn about becoming involved in more stable relationships (Auslander, Short, Succop, & Rosenthal, 2009). Greater sensitivity and dependence are encouraged among females, which may be needed for their adaptive psychosocial functioning (Gilligan, 1982).

The current study advances previous findings by suggesting that body image is very important for males (Jones & Crawford, 2005). Only body image at the age of 17 explained romantic attachment 8 years later. The different pathways found for males and females found in the current study may be attributed to the nature of romantic relationships during emerging adulthood with its steady but not fully committed quality (Shulman & Connolly, 2013). This condition probably fits more for men (Shulman, Scharf, Livne, & Barr, 2013). Our finding may also echo some evolutionary gender difference. Young men's romantic experiences tend to be defined by lust, objectification and a pursuit of sexual gratification (Kindlon & Thompson, 1999). This can explain why only body image predicted lower avoidance in their romantic encounter among males. In contrast, women place greater value on intimacy and support in their relationships (Jordan, 2004). A supportive atmosphere provided by both parents was helpful for females to develop a more adaptive body image. Moreover, unlike among males, the supportive experiences with parents accounted for the quality of females' romantic attachment.

Limitations

Although this study has its strengths, particularly the longitudinal design and the incorporation of previously understudied variables, some limitations should be noted. First, despite the significant associations over a span of 11 years, coefficients were quite low. These low path coefficient suggest the need to replicate our findings. Second, our sample consisted primarily of German individuals, which limits our ability to generalize our findings. Culture, particularly as it pertains to racial and ethnic backgrounds, can play an integral role in the development of body image. The standards for attractiveness, romantic involvement and romantic relationship quality have been shown to differ across cultural and ethnic groups (Kelly et al., 2005; Seiffge-Krenke et al., 2010). Moreover, only heterosexual romantic relationships in this study were investigated (among both parents and children). The results may not translate to same-sex relationships. Thus, future studies should aim to longitudinally replicate our findings using more diverse samples. Other factors to investigate are the role of friends and peers (Webb & Zimmer-Gembeck, 2014) and the impact of stress, which has been found to negatively influence body image (Murray et al., 2011).

Conclusions and Implications

So much attention has been given to studying how negative family factors can encourage body dissatisfaction that the potential, positive influence of the family has been somewhat overlooked. Our results indicate that a positive family climate has a significant role in establishing a positive body image in daughters, which in turn serves as a protective factor in buffering against avoidance in later adult romantic relationships. In contrast, fathers' negativity can be regarded as a risk factor for adolescent daughters. These findings suggest that more prevention and intervention work should be directed at exploiting these protective factors (e.g., the combined influence of a positive family climate and body image). In parallel, parental education about the role of a positive body image (i.e., as it relates to perceived attractiveness, physical strength, and positive body feelings) for their children's development might be warranted, because too many parents narrowly focus on negative aspects, such as eating behaviours and weight control.

REFERENCES

Abbott, B. D., & Barber, B. L. (2010). Embodied image: Gender differences in functional and aesthetic body image among Australian adolescents. *Body Image*, *7*, 22–31. doi:10.1016/j.bodyim.2009.10.004

Auslander, B. A., Short, M. B., Succop, P. A., & Rosenthal, S. L. (2009). Associations between parenting behaviors and adolescent romantic relationships. *Journal of Adolescent Health*, *45*, 98–101. doi:10.1016/j.jadohealth.2008.12.014

Blodgett Salafia, E. H., & Gondoli, D. M. (2011). A 4-year longitudinal investigation of the processes by which parents and peers influence the development of early adolescent girls' bulimic symptoms. *Journal of Early Adolescence*, *31*, 390–414. doi:10.1177/0272431610366248

Brennan, K. A., Clark, C. L., & Shaver, P. L. (1998). Self-report measurement of adult attachment: An integrative overview. In J. A. Simpson & W. S. Rholes (Eds.), *Attachment theory and close relationships* (pp. 46–76). New York, NY: Guilford Press.

Brown, B. B. (1999). 'You're going out with whom?' Peer group influences on adolescent romantic relationships. In W. Furman, B. B. Brown, & C. Feiring (Eds.), *The development of romantic relationships in adolescence* (pp. 291–329). Cambridge: Cambridge University Press.

Bucx, F., & Seiffge-Krenke, I. (2010). Romantic relationships in intra-ethnic and inter-ethnic adolescent couples in Germany: The role of attachment to parents, self-esteem, and conflict resolution skills. *International Journal of Behavioral Development*, *34*, 128–135. doi:10.1177/0165025409360294

Collins, W. A., & Van Dulmen, M. (2006). 'The course of true love(s) . . . ': Origins and pathways in the development of romantic relationships. In A. C. Crouter & A. Booth (Eds.), *Romance and sex in adolescence and emerging adulthood: Risks and opportunities* (pp. 63–86). Mahwah, NJ: Lawrence Erlbaum Associates.

Collins, W. A., Welsh, D. P., & Furman, W. (2009). Adolescent romantic relationships. *Annual Review of Psychology*, *60*, 631–652. doi:10.1146/annurev.psych.60.110707.163459

Compian, L., Gowen, L. K., & Hayward, C. (2004). Peripubertal girls' romantic and platonic involvement with boys: Associations with body image and depression symptoms. *Journal of Research on Adolescence, 14*, 23–47. doi:10.1111/j.1532-7795.2004.01401002.x

Connolly, J. A., & McIsaac, C. (2009). Romantic relationships in adolescence. In R. M. Lerner & L. Steinberg (Eds.), *Handbook of adolescent psychology, Vol. 2: Contextual influences on adolescent development* (3rd ed., pp. 104–151). Hoboken, NJ: Wiley.

Cromley, T., Neumark-Sztainer, D., Story, M., & Boutelle, K. N. (2010). Parent and family associations with weight-related behaviors and cognitions among overweight adolescents. *Journal of Adolescent Health, 47*, 263–269. doi:10.1016/j.jadohealth.2010.02.009

Dalton III, W. T., Frick-Horbury, D., & Kitzmann, K. (2006). Young adults' retrospective reports of parenting by mothers and fathers: Associations with current relationship quality. *Journal of General Psychology, 133*, 5–18. doi:10.3200/GENP.133.1.5-18

Davison, T. E., & McCabe, M. P. (2006). Adolescent body image and psychosocial functioning. *Journal of Social Psychology, 146*, 15–30. doi:10.3200/SOCP.146.1.15-30

Deusinger, I. M. (1998). *Die Frankfurter Körperkonzeptskalen (FKKS).* Handanweisung mit Bericht über vielfältige Validierungsstudien [The Frankfurter body concept scales: Manual with validation studies]. Göttingen: Hogrefe.

Engels, R. C. M. E., Finkenauer, C., Meeus, W., & Dekovic, M. (2001). Parental attachment and adolescents' emotional adjustment: The associations with social skills and relational competence. *Journal of Counseling Psychology, 48*, 428–439. doi:10.1037/0022-0167.48.4.428

Feldman, S. S., Gowen, L. K., & Fisher, L. (1998). Family relationships and gender as predictors of romantic intimacy in young adults: A longitudinal study. *Journal of Research on Adolescence, 8*, 263–286. doi:10.1207/s15327795jra0802_5

Furman, W., & Buhrmester, D. (1985). Children's perceptions of the personal relationships in their social networks. *Developmental Psychology, 21*, 1016–1024. doi:10.1037/0012-1649.21.6.1016

Furman, W., & Shomaker, L. B. (2008). Patterns of interaction in adolescent romantic relationships: Distinct features and links to other close relationships. *Journal of Adolescence, 31*, 771–788. doi:10.1016/j.adolescence.2007.10.007

Furman, W., Simon, V. A., Shaffer, L., & Bouchey, H. A. (2002). Adolescents' working models and styles for relationships with parents, friends, and romantic partners. *Child Development, 73*, 241–255. doi:10.1111/1467-8624.00403

Furman, W., & Wehner, E. A. (1997). Adolescent romantic relationships: A developmental perspective. In S. Shulman & W. A. Collins (Eds.), *Romantic relationships in adolescence: Developmental perspectives* (pp. 168–195). San Francisco, CA: Jossey-Bass.

Furman, W., & Winkles, J. K. (2010). Predicting romantic involvement, relationship cognitions, and relationship qualities from physical appearance, perceived norms, and relational styles regarding friends and parents. *Journal of Adolescence, 33*, 827–836. doi:10.1016/j.adolescence.2010.07.004

Gilligan, C. (1982). *In a different voice*. Cambridge, MA: Harvard University Press.

Gray, M. R., & Steinberg, L. (1999). Adolescent romance and the parent–child relationship: A contextual perspective. In C. Feiring, W. Furman, & B. B. Brown (Eds.), *The development of romantic relationships in adolescence* (pp. 235–262). New York, NY: Cambridge University Press.

Halpern, C., King, R. B., Oslak, S. G., & Udry, J. R. (2005). Body mass index, dieting, romance, and sexual activity in adolescent girls: Relationships over time. *Journal of Research on Adolescence, 15*, 535–559. doi:10.1111/j.1532-7795.2005.00110.x

Hazan, C., & Shaver, P. (1987). Romantic love conceptualized as an attachment process. *Journal of Personality and Social Psychology, 52*, 511–524. doi:10.1037/0022-3514.52.3.511

Helfert, S., & Warschburger, P. (2011). A prospective study on the impact of peer and parental pressure on body dissatisfaction in adolescent girls and boys. *Body Image, 8*, 101–109. doi:10.1016/j.bodyim.2011.01.004

Hu, L., & Bentler, P. (1999). Cutoff criteria for fit indexes in covariance structure analysis: Conventional criteria versus new alternatives. *Structural Equation Modeling, 6*(1), 1–55. doi:10.1080/10705519909540118

Jones, D., & Crawford, J. K. (2005). Adolescent boys and body image: Weight and muscularity concerns as dual pathways to body dissatisfaction. *Journal of Youth and Adolescence, 34*, 629–636. doi:10.1007/s10964-005-8951-3

Jordan, J. V. (2004). Toward competence and connection. In J. V. Jordan, M. Walker, & L. M. Hartling (Eds.), *The complexity of connection: Writings from the Stone Center's Jean Baker Miller Training Institute* (pp. 11–27). New York, NY: Guilford Press.

Kan, M. L., McHale, S. M., & Crouter, A. C. (2008). Parental involvement in adolescent romantic relationships: Patterns and correlates. *Journal of Youth and Adolescence, 37*, 168–179. doi:10.1007/s10964-007-9185-3

Kelly, A. M., Wall, M., Eisenberg, M. E., Story, M., & Neumark-Sztainer, D. (2005). Adolescent girls with high body satisfaction: Who are they and what can they teach us?. *Journal of Adolescent Health, 37*, 391–396. doi:10.1016/j.jadohealth.2004.08.008

Kim, H. K., & Capaldi, D. M. (2004). The association of antisocial behavior and depressive symptoms between partners and risk for aggression in romantic relationships. *Journal of Family Psychology, 18*, 82–96. doi:10.1037/0893-3200.18.1.82

Kindlon, D., & Thompson, M. (1999). *Raising cain: Protecting the emotional life of boys*. New York, NY: Ballantine.

Laufer, M. L., & Laufer, E. (1984). *Adolescence and developmental breakdown*. Yale: New Haven.

Madsen, S. D. (2008). Parents' management of adolescents' romantic relationships through dating rules: Gender variations and correlates of relationship qualities. *Journal of Youth and Adolescence, 37*, 1044–1058. doi:doi:10.1007/s10964-008-9313-8

Mayseless, O., Wiseman, H., & Hai, I. (1998). Adolescents' relationships with father, mother, and same-gender friend. *Journal of Adolescent Research, 13*, 101–123. doi:10.1177/0743554898131006

McCabe, M. P., & Ricciardelli, L. A. (2005). A prospective study of pressures from parents, peers, and the media on extreme weight change behaviors among adolescent boys and girls. *Behaviour Research and Therapy, 43*, 653–668. doi:10.1016/j.brat.2004.05.004

Murray, K. M., Byrne, D. G., & Rieger, E. (2011). Investigating adolescent stress and body image. *Journal of Adolescence, 34*, 269–278. doi:10.1016/j.adolescence.2010.05.004

Muthén, L. K., & Muthén, B. O. (2010). *Mplus – Statistical analysis with latent variables*. Los Angeles, CA: Muthén & Muthén.

Rosenblum, G. D., & Lewis, M. (1999). The relations among body image, physical attractiveness, and body mass in adolescence. *Child Development, 70*, 50–64. doi:10.1111/1467-8624.00005

Scharf, M., & Mayseless, O. (2008). Late adolescent girls' relationships with parents and romantic partner: The distinct role of mothers and fathers. *Journal of Adolescence, 31*, 837–855. doi:10.1016/j.adolescence.2008.06.012

Seiffe-Krenke, I. (2006). Leaving home or still in the nest? Parent–child relationships and psychological health as predictors of different leaving home patterns. *Developmental Psychology, 42*, 864–876. doi:10.1037/0012-1649.42.5.864

Seiffge-Krenke, I. (2003). Testing theories of romantic development from adolescence to young adulthood: Evidence of a developmental sequence. *International Journal of Behavioral Development, 27*, 519–531. doi:10.1080/01650250344000145

Seiffge-Krenke, I., Bosma, H., Chau, C., Cok, F., Gillespie, C., Loncaric, D., … Rohail, I. (2010). All they need is love? Placing romantic stress in the context of other stressors: A 17-nation study. *International Journal of Behavioral Development, 34*, 106–112. doi:10.1177/0165025409360290

Seiffge-Krenke, I., Overbeek, G., & Vermulst, A. (2010). Parent–child relationship trajectories during adolescence: Longitudinal associations with romantic outcomes in emerging adulthood. *Journal of Adolescence, 33*, 159–171. doi:10.1016/j.adolescence.2009.04.001

Seiffge-Krenke, I., & Shulman, S. (2012). Transformation in heterosexual romantic relationships across the transition into adolescence. In B. Laursen & W. A. Collins (Eds.), *Relationship pathways: From adolescence to young adulthood* (pp. 191–214). Thousand Oaks, CA: Sage.

Seiffge-Krenke, I., Shulman, S., & Kiessinger, N. (2001). Adolescent precursors of romantic relationships in young adulthood. *Journal of Social and Personal Relationships*, *18*, 327–346. doi:10.1177/0265407501183002

Shulman, S., & Connolly, J. (2013). The challenge of romantic relationships in emerging adulthood: Reconceptualization of the field. *Emerging Adulthood*, *1*, 27–39. doi:10.1177/2167696812467330

Shulman, S., & Scharf, M. (2000). Adolescent romantic behaviors and perceptions: Age- and gender-related differences, and links with family and peer relationships. *Journal of Research on Adolescence*, *10*, 99–118. doi:10.1207/SJRA1001_5

Shulman, S., Scharf, M, Livne, Y., & Barr, T. (2013). Patterns of romantic involvement among emerging adults: Psychosocial correlates and precursors. *International Journal of Behavioral Development*, *37*, 460–467. doi:10.1177/0165025413491371

Shulman, S., & Seiffge-Krenke, I. (1997). *Fathers and adolescents. Developmental and clinical perspectives*. London: Routledge.

Shulman, S., Walsh, S. D., Weisman, O., & Schelyer, M. (2009). Romantic contexts, sexual behavior, and depressive symptoms among adolescent males and females. *Sex Roles*, *61*, 850–863. doi:10.1007/s11199-009-9691-8

Simon, V. A., Aikins, J. W., & Prinstein, M. J. (2008). Romantic partner selection and socialization during early adolescence. *Child Development*, *79*, 1676–1692. doi:10.1111/j.1467-8624.2008.01218.x

Snary, J. (1993). *How fathers care for the next generation*. Cambridge, MA: Harvard University Press.

Statistisches Bundesamt. (2013). *Bildung und Kultur* [Education and culture]. Wiesbaden: Statistisches Bundesamt.

Stice, E., & Whitenton, K. (2002). Risk factors for body dissatisfaction in adolescent girls: A longitudinal investigation. *Developmental Psychology*, *38*, 669–678. doi:10.1037/0012-1649.38.5.669

Webb, H. J., & Zimmer-Gembeck, M. J. (2014). The role of friends and peers in adolescent body dissatisfaction: A review and critique of 15 years of research. *Journal of Research on Adolescence*, *24*, 564–590. doi:10.1111/jora.12084

Wood-Barcalow, N. L., Tylka, T. L., & Augustus-Horvath, C. L. (2010). But I like my body: Positive body image characteristics and a holistic model for young-adult women. *Body Image*, *7*, 106–116. doi:10.1016/j.bodyim.2010.01.001

Adolescents' use of affiliative and aggressive strategies during conflict with romantic partners and best-friends

Jennifer Connolly[1], Kyla Baird[1], Valeriya Bravo[1], Benedicte Lovald[1], Debra Pepler[1], and Wendy Craig[2]

[1]Department of Psychology, York University, Toronto, Canada
[2]Department of Psychology, Queen's University, Kingston, Canada

Objective: Developmental theory suggests romantic relationships present unique demands when adolescents transition from the interaction patterns of same-sex friendships to cross-gender interactions. A possible response is to incorporate behaviours of the other gender: girls adopting aggressive strategies and boys adopting affiliative ones. The goal of this study is to explore this hypothesis by comparing conflict resolution among romantic couples and same-sex best friends. **Method**: Observational methods were employed with 37 female best friends, 22 male best friends and 37 romantic couples. Of the romantic couples, 35 also were observed with a best friend. Affiliative and aggressive behaviours were tabulated during two conflict tasks. **Results**: Female best friends were more affiliative than male best friends and romantic partners; these latter dyads were more aggressive than the female best friends. Within group comparisons indicated that boys and girls decreased their affiliative behaviours, especially verbal humour, and increased their aggressive behaviours, especially teasing, when observed with the romantic partner compared to the best friend. Decomposing the romantic dyad, girlfriends displayed relatively more aggressive behaviours than their boyfriends, and boyfriends exhibited more affiliative behaviours. **Conclusions**: Findings shed light on gendered shifts in patterns of interaction as adolescents transition from same-sex friendships to romantic relationships.

The emergence of romantic relationships is one of the defining features of adolescence (Connolly & McIsaac, 2011). Alongside their intrinsic fascination,

No potential conflict of interest was reported by the authors.

adolescent dating presents a range of challenges. Prominent among these is negotiating conflicts. From a developmental perspective (Maccoby, 1998), gender-specific interaction styles previously acquired in same-sex friendships do not fully prepare adolescents to negotiate conflict with cross-gender partners (Underwood & Rosen, 2009). How youth adapt to the changing relationship contexts of friends and romantic partners is largely unknown (Furman & Rose, 2015). Gender developmental and social exchange theories suggest that youth may respond to these challenges by incorporating elements of the other gender's behavioural style (Laursen & Jensen-Campbell, 1999). The current research compares adolescent boys' and girls' affiliative and aggressive conflict behaviours in romantic and friendship contexts.

CONFLICT IN SAME-SEX FRIENDSHIPS AND ROMANTIC RELATIONSHIPS

Conflicts in close relationships are largely unavoidable (Furman & Shomaker, 2008). While girls' same-sex friendships are less conflictual than those of boys, both genders must learn strategies to resolve disagreements (Brendgen, Markiewicz, Doyle, & Bukowski, 2001). Girls generally approach same-sex friends with an affiliative orientation and strive to preserve harmony in the relationship (Keener, Strough, & DiDonato, 2012; Rose & Rudolph, 2006). When conflict arises, girls typically use reduction strategies and express their disagreements indirectly (Maccoby, 1998). In contrast, boys' interactional style with same-sex friends is agentic in orientation, focusing on dominance and power (Giordano, Longmore, & Manning, 2006; Keener et al., 2012). They tend to respond to conflict with unilateral or restrictive actions and with the use of aggressive behaviours (Maccoby, 1998; Underwood & Rosen, 2009). Despite these differences, the voluntary nature of friendships prioritizes conflict strategies that preserve the relationship (Adams & Laursen, 2001).

Adolescents' same-sex friendships are a critical background to their emerging romantic relationships (Connolly, Craig, Goldberg, & Pepler, 2004; Connolly, Furman, & Konarski, 2000). Alongside other contributions, same-sex friendships provide guidelines for romantic conflict resolution (Laursen, 1993). These may be seen as especially helpful because romantic relationships and friendships are both voluntary and egalitarian, meaning both individuals are motivated to maintain the relationship and prevent dissolution by engaging in behaviour that promotes mutuality (Adams & Laursen, 2001; Shulman & Laursen, 2002; Shulman, Tuval-Mashiach, Levran, & Anbar, 2006). However, incongruences in friendship-based conflict strategies may impact adolescents' understanding of various events in their romantic relationships (Galliher, Welsh, Rostosky, & Kawaguchi, 2004). Heterosexual romantic relationships present the unique challenge of solving conflict with a partner of the opposite gender, and not all gender-consolidated conflict strategies will be helpful (Keener et al., 2012).

Theorists have debated how the conflict strategies acquired in same-sex friendships might be transferred to romantic relationships. From a social learning perspective, same-sex conflict strategies should be transferred directly to romantic relationships. However, available evidence does not support this pathway since adolescents have been shown to modify their conflict strategies across other relationships, namely peers and parents (Adams & Laursen, 2001; Jensen-Campbell, Graziano, & Hair, 1996; Shute & Charlton, 2006). Alternatively, gender developmental and social exchange theories suggest that adolescent boys and girls adapt their same-sex conflict strategies to fit the new context of a romantic relationship. The social exchange theory posits that adolescents are highly motivated to maximize the amicable benefits of their romantic relationship and will modify their behaviours to achieve this end (Laursen & Williams, 1997). Gender developmental theory (Maccoby, 2002) proposes that adolescents modify some elements of their gender-solidified strategies by adopting elements of the other gender's conflict strategies. Consistent with these theories, we would expect that, in contrast to conflict approaches in same-sex friendships, boys should demonstrate more affiliative behaviours and girls demonstrate more aggressive behaviours in the context of a romantic relationship.

While research is limited, the available evidence is supportive of these hypotheses. One study, comparing the self-reported conflict strategies with friends and romantic partners, found that adolescent girls reported more anger with their partners as compared to boys (Shute & Charlton, 2006). A study of adult couples reported a gendered switch in everyday behaviour based on the context of the relationship, although the study did not include conflict situations specifically (Suh, Moskowitz, Fournier, & Zuroff, 2004). Research examining conflict in adolescent romantic couples has shown gendered conflict styles within the dyad. For example, Rose and Rudolph (2006) have demonstrated that girlfriends are more likely to communicate their view of the problem than are boyfriends. Girlfriends are also more likely to express negative emotions (Creasey & Hesson-McInnis, 2001) and to criticize their partner (Shulman et al., 2006). These studies support a more confrontational style for girls with their boyfriends, which is consistent with the adaptation hypotheses derived from gendered developmental and social exchange theories.

AGGRESSIVE AND AFFILIATIVE CONFLICT STRATEGIES

Conflict strategies are an important area of consideration, as conflict undermines mental health and relationship quality (Ha, Dishion, Overbeek, Burk, & Engels, 2014; Hill & Peplau, 1998). The current study examines gender differences in the use of aggressive and affiliative behaviours when negotiating conflict with same-sex friends and romantic partners. In the aggressive domain, we focus on direct aggression, mock aggression and teasing. In the affiliative domain, we focus on affection and humour.

In the context of conflict, adolescents can use aggressive behaviours intended to harm the other person (Laursen, Finkelstein, & Betts, 2001). Verbal hostility is most common although physical acts can also occur. Mock aggression differs from direct aggression because it co-occurs with clear signs of playful intent, typically shown by smiles and positive affect (Pellegrini, 2003). Somewhat similar to mock aggression, teasing pairs intentional provocations with playfulness (Keltner, Capps, Kring, Young, & Heerey, 2001). Teasing differs in its reduced level of provocation, with mock aggression being more derisive and extreme. Aggression, teasing and mock aggression are predominantly male forms of conflict behaviour (Mooney, Creeser, & Blatchford, 1991; Maccoby, 1990; Pellegrini, 2003).

During conflict, affiliative exchanges also occur, aiming to reduce tension (Campbell, Martin, & Ward, 2008; Driver & Gottman, 2004). Affection can include verbal and physical forms of communicating caring, support and positive regard, as well as expressions of empathy and validation. Humour is manifested in good-natured playfulness wherein the positive intent of amusing the partner is evident through such actions as joking, animated gesturing or adopting a funny voice to express their wit. Given girls' orientation towards prosocial, collaborative and egalitarian behaviours (Keener et al., 2012), it is presumed these affiliative exchanges of humour, physical and verbal affection, will be most prominent among girls.

THE PRESENT STUDY

Given the complexity of adolescent relationship dynamics, researchers have highlighted the value of observational methodologies (Ha et al., 2014; Ha et al., 2013; Simon & Furman, 2010; Welsh & Shulman, 2008). Accordingly, we observe adolescent girls and boys negotiating conflict with romantic partners and same-sex best friends. Using between-group and within-group samples, we compare affiliative and aggressive strategies in romantic couples, male best friends and female best friends. We expect romantic dyads to be more similar to male best friends on aggressive behaviours and more similar to female best friends on affiliative behaviours. We also compare affiliative and aggressive behaviours of boyfriends and girlfriends within the romantic dyad. We expect boyfriends to score higher on affiliative behaviours and girlfriends to score higher on aggressive behaviours.

METHOD

Participants

The participants included 60 girls and 36 boys aged 15–18 years ($M = 16.33$, $SD = 0.52$). Sample characteristics are shown in Table 1. Participants completed

TABLE 1
Characteristics of sample ($n = 96$)

	Mean (SD)	*Percentage (%)*
Age		
Male	16.34 (0.54)	
Female	16.33 (0.51)	
Race		
European–Canadian		76
Asian–Canadian		7
African/Caribbean Canadian		3
South Asian–Canadian		3
Other or mixed		11
Living configuration		
Living with both biological parents		69
Living with mother only		18
Other family configurations		13

a social network checklist. They were eligible for the study if they reported a same-sex best friend and a current romantic partner. However, at the time of the observation many eligible adolescents did not bring their romantic partner. Of the 96 students, 59 participated with best friend only (37 females; 22 males), 2 participated with romantic partner only (1 female, 1 male) and 35 participated with a romantic partner and a best friend (22 females, 13 males). Participants with both relationship types comprised the within-group sample. To take advantage of the full participant pool, a between-group sample was generated by deleting the best-friend observations of adolescents with both dyad types and pooling them with the two adolescents with only a romantic partner observation. As such, three groups of mutually exclusive dyads were created; 37 romantic couples, 37 female best friends and 22 male best friends. In the between-group analysis, participants in the three dyads did not differ on age, χ^2 $(2, N = 93) = .49, p = .62$, ethnicity (European–Canadian versus Other), χ^2 $(2, N = 93) = .59, p = .74$, or family composition (intact versus not intact), χ^2 $(2, N = 93) = 2.19, p = .33$. They differed in relationship duration, $t\,(82) = -.37, p < .001$. Friendships averaged 61.14 months ($SD = 40.18$) and romantic relationships averaged 15.82 months ($SD = 14.19$).

Procedure

The observation started with a five-minute warm-up activity wherein the adolescents planned a party for their friends. Participants then engaged in two 7-min conflict discussions. Using a modified version of the revealed differences task (Knox, 1971), personally relevant topics were selected from a list that included themes of jealousy, competition, neglect, disliking friends, trust and peer pressure.

The order of discussion topics alternated between target adolescent and his/her partner across participants, yielding a counterbalanced design. The interactions were videotaped in participants' homes or in some cases, in a private location at their school. The researchers monitored the interactions from a nearby location.

Observational coding

The behaviours of each member of the dyad were coded separately as the frequency of occurrence per minute for affiliative and aggressive categories. Definitions were drawn from the Specific Affect Coding System (SPAFF; Gottman, 1994; Jones, Carrere, & Gottman, 2005) and the Peer Process Code (PPC; Dishion et al., 1989).

The aggressive domain included verbal aggression (physical aggression was initially coded but occurred too infrequently to retain), teasing and mock aggression. *Verbal aggression* was defined as hostile verbalizations (e.g., name calling, threats, insults, swearing) expressed with neutral or negative affect with the intent of humiliating, denigrating or upsetting the partner. *Verbal teasing* was defined as playful provocations directed at the partner (e.g., playfully blaming or disapproving of partner, playful competition) and were always accompanied by playful affect (e.g., smiles, laughter). *Physical teasing* included playful physical provocations accompanied by smiles or laughter (e.g., physically imitating the partner, animated facial expressions or gestures used to make fun of the partner). *Verbal mock aggression* captured partner-directed contemptuous verbalizations (e.g., name calling, threats, insults, swearing) paired with positive affect. Verbal mock aggression was distinguished from verbal teasing by its markedly derisive content. *Physical mock aggression* was defined as the pairing of distinctly aggressive physical behaviours (e.g., hit, push, slap, poke, hit with object) with clear indicators of positive affect.

The affiliative domain included humour and affection. *Verbal humour* was defined as good-natured joking (e.g., speaking in a funny voice, exaggerated or imitative expressions, private jokes). *Physical humour* was defined as positive physical play (e.g., making funny faces, animated gesturing). Behaviours coded as humour were characterized by positive intent (to make partner laugh) and never employed at the partner's expense. *Verbal affection* included warm, caring verbalizations directed at the partner that communicated positive feelings, approval, expressions of empathy, validation and support. *Physical affection* included physical touch or gesturing that showed affection, caring or support for the partner (e.g., hand holding, hugging, kissing, "high fives", "thumbs up").

To analyse differences across the three relationships, dyad scores were computed for each behaviour, calculated as the total number of times the behaviour was exhibited by both partners across the two observation tasks. Two summary scores were also computed: affiliative behaviours (verbal affection, physical affection, verbal humour, physical humour) and aggressive behaviours (verbal teasing, physical teasing, verbal mock aggression, physical mock aggression and verbal aggression). To control for varying base rates of activity between dyad types, the summary scores were computed as proportions of total behaviours. To compare differences within romantic dyads, individual boyfriend and girlfriend scores were computed.

Inter-rater reliability

Prior to coding, three observers were trained by the first author until they reached a minimum agreement of 70%. Coding reliability was reviewed weekly to detect and prevent observer drift. Following completion of the coding, inter-rater reliability was determined for 20% of the observations; coders were blind to which observations were utilized. Inter-rater agreement was as follows: verbal affection (93.51%); physical affection (99.32%); verbal humour (70.87%); physical humour (95.15%); verbal teasing (78.21%); physical teasing (98.10%); verbal mock aggression (96.21%); physical mock aggression (99.39%); verbal aggression (96.13%). Inter-rater agreement of 70% or higher is considered acceptable (Multon, 2010). All disagreements were reviewed and a consensus code was assigned.

RESULTS

Preliminary analyses

Variable distributions were screened for normality and all conflict variables were transformed to correct for positive skewness. Variable frequencies did not differ significantly between the two conflict discussion tasks, $F(1, 92) = 1.88, p = .17$. Selector of topic had no effect on 16 of 18 behaviours, (F (2, 87) values range from .01 to 2.68, *p*s range from .99 to .08). Physical affection in discussion 1 and verbal mock aggression in discussion 2 were more frequent when the target selected the topic ($F(2, 87) = 3.93, p = .023, \eta_p^2 = .083$ and $F(2, 75) = 4.03, p = .02, \eta_p^2 = .10$, respectively).

Correlations among conflict behaviours were computed (see Table 2). Moderate correlations within affiliative and aggressive behaviours were obtained, providing support for our use of summary scores. Correlations across aggressive and affiliative behaviours were largely non-significant, with the exception of physical affection which was significantly correlated with verbal teasing, mock aggression and verbal aggression. Affiliative and aggressive summary scores were not significantly correlated, $r(96) = .10, p = .34$.

Comparing romantic partners and best friends

To assess whether romantic and best friend dyads used similar or different conflict tactics, comparisons were undertaken of the mean frequencies of

TABLE 2
Correlations among affiliative and aggressive conflict behaviours

	1	*2*	*3*	*4*	*5*	*6*	*7*	*8*
Affiliative								
1. Verbal affection	–							
2. Physical affection	.22*							
3. Verbal humour	−.09	.08						
4. Physical humour	−.10	.18	.55**					
Aggressive								
5. Verbal teasing	−.04	.23*	.05	.11				
6. Physical teasing	−.08	.18	−.06	.08	.41**			
7. Verbal mock aggression	−.03	.21*	.17	.15	.60**	.38**		
8. Physical mock aggression	.04	.36**	.05	.21*	.41**	.50**	.48**	
9. Verbal aggression	.01	.26**	−.18	.01	.25*	.36**	.37**	.30**

***$p < .001$. **$p < .01$. *$p < .05$.

individual behaviours and the summary scores. Between-group comparisons of the dyad scores for romantic couples, male best friends and female best friends, were performed using ANOVAS followed by pairwise comparisons (see Table 3). Within-group comparisons of the subset of adolescents who participated with both romantic partner and best friend were performed using paired *t*-tests of the boys and girls separately (see Table 4).

Affiliative behaviours. The between-group comparisons revealed significant differences for verbal humour, F (2, 93) = 14.28, $p < .001$, $\eta_p^2 = .24$ and

TABLE 3
Mean frequencies of dyadic conflict behaviours for romantic couples and best friends—between-group sample

Observed variables	*Romantic couples*[c]	*Female best friends*[d]	*Male best friends*[e]
Affiliative behaviours			
Verbal affection	2.66 (2.76)	2.95 (3.57)	1.09 (1.23)
Physical affection	2.26[a] (6.16)	0.51 (1.40)	0.13[a] (0.46)
Verbal humour	12.82[a,b] (12.69)	30.30[a] (18.05)	25.18[b] (21.24)
Physical humour	1.29 (1.71)	2.81 (3.05)	2.50 (5.61)
Aggressive behaviours			
Verbal teasing	13.77 [a] (12.67)	7.35[b] (7.27)	13.45 (12.44)
Physical teasing	1.66 [a] (2.71)	0.46[a,b] (1.01)	2.09[b] (2.97)
Verbal mock aggression	1.29 (2.59)	0.43[a] (1.01)	2.86[a] (5.46)
Physical mock aggression	.89 (2.30)	0.14 (0.34)	0.55 (1.37)
Verbal aggression	.97 (3.08)	0.32 (1.38)	0.55 (1.79)
Proportion scores			
Total affiliation/total behaviours	.55 [a] (.26)	0.81[a,b] (0.16)	0.63[b] (0.22)
Total aggression/total behaviours	.45 [a] (.26)	0.19[a,b] (0.16)	0.37[b] (0.22)

[a,b]Denote significant contrasts ($ps < .05$). [c]$n = 37$. [d]$n = 37$. [e]$n = 22$.

TABLE 4

Mean frequencies for dyadic conflict behaviours of romantic couples and best friends—within-group sample

	Boys[c]		Girls[d]	
Observed variables	*Romantic couples*	*Best friends*	*Romantic couples*	*Best friends*
Affiliative behaviours				
Verbal affection	2.77 (2.55)	1.15 (1.07)	2.59 (2.94)	2.95 (3.54)
Physical affection	.38 (.87)	.54 (1.33)	3.36 (7.58) [a]	.14 (.35) [b]
Verbal humour	10.54 (6.55) [a]	29.31 (13.65) [b]	14.18 (15.21) [a]	24.09 (11.43) [b]
Physical humour	1.23 (1.48)	4.54 (5.49)	1.32 (1.86)	1.32 (1.46)
Aggressive behaviours				
Verbal teasing	16.15 (16.28) [a]	6.69 (8.64) [b]	12.36 (10.14) [a]	5.23 (6.61) [b]
Physical teasing	2.61 (3.76)	.85 (1.34)	1.09 (1.69)	1.09 (2.43)
Verbal mock aggression	2.31 (3.25)	1.46 (2.50)	.68 (1.96)	.36 (.79)
Physical mock aggression	1.38 (3.23)	.31 (.63)	.59 (1.53)	.18 (.50)
Verbal aggression	1.62 (4.66)	.15 (.55)	.59 (1.59)	.09 (.29)
Proportion scores				
Total affiliation/total behaviours	.48 (.24) [a]	.84 (.18) [b]	.60 (.27) [a]	.82 (.19) [b]
Total aggression/total behaviours	.52 (.24) [a]	.16 (.18) [b]	.40 (.27) [a]	.18 (.19) [b]

[a,b]Denote significant difference (*ps* $< .05$) between romantic couples and best friends compared within gender. [c]$n = 13$. [d]$n = 22$.

physical affection, F (2, 93) = 3.32, $p = .04$, $\eta_p^2 = .07$. Male best-friend dyads and female best-friend dyads used more verbal humour than romantic partners. On the other hand, physical affection was more frequent between romantic partners than between male best friends, while similar to the level observed for female best friends.

The within-group comparisons revealed that, for both boys and girls, there was a significant reduction in the use of verbal humour within the romantic partnership compared to best friends; boys t (12) = 4.69, $p = .001$, $d = 1.89$, girls t (21) = 3.14, $p = .005$, $d = .94$. Girls, but not boys, used significantly more physical affection with their romantic partners compared to their best friends, t (21) = −2.34, $p = .03$, $d = -.74$.

Aggressive behaviours. The between-group comparisons revealed significant differences between dyads for physical teasing F (2, 93) = 6.06, $p < .01$, $\eta_p^2 = .12$, verbal mock aggression, F (2, 93) = 4.65, $p = .01$, $\eta_p^2 = .09$ and verbal teasing, F (2, 93) = 3.29, $p = .04$, $\eta_p^2 = .07$. Romantic partners and male best friends were similar in their use of physical and verbal teasing and exhibited significantly more of these behaviours than female best friends. Male best friends employed significantly more verbal mock aggression than female best friends, while romantic couple use did not differ significantly from either friendship.

The within-group comparisons revealed a significant difference in verbal teasing for both boys and girls: boys t (12) = −4.29, $p = .001$, $d = -0.87$, and girls t (21) = −2.43, $p = .03$, $d = -0.83$. Higher rates of verbal teasing were observed in romantic dyads compared to best friends.

Affiliative and aggressive summary scores. The between-group comparisons revealed significant differences for both summary scores, F (2, 95) = 14.56, $p < .001$, $\eta_p^2 = .24$. Female best friends displayed higher proportion of affiliative behaviours compared to romantic partners and male best friends, whereas the latter two groups had higher proportion of aggressive behaviours.

The within-group comparisons demonstrated that both boys and girls used significantly less affiliative and more aggressive behaviours with romantic partners than best friends (boys t (12) = ±5.58, $p < .001$, $d = \pm 1.71$, girls t (21) = ±3.06, $p = .01$, $d = \pm 0.97$).

Comparing boyfriends and girlfriends in the romantic dyad

To assess whether boyfriends and girlfriends used similar or different conflict tactics, repeated measures ANOVAS were undertaken (see Table 5). Because relationship duration varied across romantic dyads, we considered whether this variable could be a moderator of differences between boyfriends and girlfriends. Pearson correlations were computed between relationship duration and conflict behaviour, separately for boys and girls. Of the 18 correlations, significant effects were found for verbal teasing (female r (36) = .44, $p <$ 01; male r (36) = .42, $p < .02$) and verbal mock aggression (female r (36) = .39, $p < .02$; male

TABLE 5
Mean frequencies of individual girlfriend and boyfriend conflict behaviours

	Romantic partner	
	Girlfriends	*Boyfriends*
Affiliative behaviours		
Verbal affection	1.27 (1.74)	1.30 (1.79)
Physical affection	1.22 (4.10)	0.95 (2.69)
Verbal humour	6.41 (6.79)	6.46 (6.73)
Physical humour	0.68 (1.11)	0.68 (1.08)
Aggressive behaviours		
Verbal teasing	7.41[a] (6.56)	6.05 [b] (7.47)
Physical teasing	0.68 (1.33)	1.00 (1.63)
Verbal mock aggression	1.03 (2.18)	0.46 (1.35)
Physical mock aggression	0.70 [a] (1.79)	0.22 [b] (0.53)
Verbal aggression	0.57 (2.51)	0.38 (0.98)
Proportion scores		
Total affiliation/total behaviours	0.51 [a] (0.29)	0.60 [b] (0.28)
Total aggression/total behaviours	0.49 [a] (0.29)	0.40 [b] (0.28)

[a,b]Denote significant difference ($p < .05$) between girls and boys.

r (36) = .40, $p < .02$). Consequently, duration was dichotomized at 12 months and included as a moderator in the ANOVAs. No significant interaction effects were found for any of the behaviours and so the analyses are reported without duration.

Affiliative behaviours. No significant differences were found between boyfriends' and girlfriends' use of the affiliative conflict tactics.

Aggressive behaviours. In the aggressive domain, girlfriends displayed significantly more verbal teasing, F (1, 35) = 4.19, $p = .05$, $\eta_p^2 = .107$ than their boyfriends. Girlfriends also exhibited significantly higher levels of physical mock aggression, F (1, 35) = 3.98, $p = .05$, $\eta_p^2 = .10$ than their boyfriends.

Affiliative and aggressive summary scores. Significant differences for both summary scores were found, F (1, 35) = 4.36, $p < .001$, $\eta_p^2 = .11$. Boyfriends used more affiliative behaviours, while girlfriends displayed more aggressive behaviours than their boyfriends.

DISCUSSION

This study investigated how adolescent boys and girls, with their distinct interactional styles acquired in prior same-sex friendships adapt to the challenge of negotiating conflict with heterosexual romantic partners. Gender developmental and social exchange theories (Laursen & Jensen-Campbell, 1999; Maccoby, 2002) suggest that adolescents may respond to the novel demands of romantic relationships by integrating into their repertoire, behaviours aligned with those of the other gender. Our findings showed that adolescents altered their behaviours and utilized affiliative or aggressive behaviours more typical of the other gender when resolving conflict with a romantic partner. These findings are among the first to provide support for gendered patterns of romantic interaction.

Focusing first on our comparisons of the dyads, the study provides support for gendered differences in conflict strategies among same-sex friendships. Girls with their same-sex friends used affiliative strategies when discussing conflict situations. Their behaviours with each other often exhibited conflict-mitigating tactics, including humour and expressions of caring, support and affection. In contrast, boys with their same-sex friends exhibited relatively more aggressive strategies. Their tactics tended towards playful opposition, including teasing and mock aggression. These findings are in line with the extant research that indicates girls approach their same-sex friendships with connectedness and affiliation, whereas boys' relationships are generally defined by competition, power and dominance (Giordano et al., 2006; Keener et al., 2012; Rose & Rudolph, 2006).

Importantly, our dyad comparisons revealed differences in the behaviours of male and female best friends with those of romantic partners. The findings were largely consistent with our hypotheses. Romantic dyads and male friends were similar in their overall relative use of aggressive behaviours and both were higher than the female friendships. These findings were evident when comparing the subset of adolescents with both relationship types, suggesting that boys and girls may be altering their aggressive and affiliative behaviours in the two contexts. We speculate that adolescent girls may adopt the strategy of matching the more dominant behavioural style of boys, while the boys adopt affiliative strategies in response to the more passive style of the girls. Less consistent were the findings that romantic couples were not strongly similar to female friends in affiliative behaviours. It would appear from these findings that romantic couples adapt their conflict strategies to be more like the male pattern of interaction than that of the females.

In considering these findings, it is important to note the types of aggressive behaviours which were observed. In all dyads, playful forms of aggression were evident, with virtually no direct aggression. Instead adolescents teased each other and made gestures of mock aggression. It is notable that these behaviours were positively correlated with gestures of affection. These findings are consistent with the view that pairing these playful forms of aggression with displays of positive affect communicates non-aggressive intent (Campbell et al., 2008; Driver & Gottman, 2004). Rather than increasing the conflict, these behaviours serve the goal in preserving the relationship by avoiding conflict and facilitating positive engagement with a partner.

Turning to the comparisons of boyfriends and girlfriends within the romantic couples, our findings provide further support that this novel situation draws from adolescents' patterns of behaviours which differ from their gender-consolidated styles. That is to say, in the context of discussing a conflict with their romantic partner, girlfriends showed a greater use of aggressive strategies and boyfriends showed a greater use of affiliative strategies. Here it is again important to note that girlfriends' aggression towards their boyfriends was playful in nature, specifically employing the strategies of teasing and mock aggression seen in male best friendships. Accompanying mildly aggressive acts with playful cues may have allowed girls to express frustration or disapproval of their boyfriend, without actually jeopardizing the relationship. Although we cannot be certain from the current study, it is possible that girls have observed boys' frequent use of teasing and mock aggression with their same-sex friends and boys have observed girls' successful use of affiliative behaviours with each other girls. It is possible that adolescents are more motivated to prevent conflict in the romantic relationship than in a friendship and so they will go to great lengths to avoid disagreement, including the adoption of the behavioural style of the other gender.

LIMITATIONS AND FUTURE DIRECTIONS

Findings from the current research should be considered in the context of certain limitations. The unequal distribution of dyads across relationship types, and specifically the smaller number of adolescents who brought their romantic partner to the observation, limited our use of a within-subject design to small sample *t*-tests. While the findings of the within and between analyses were very similar, it is still possible that unobserved heterogeneity between same-sex friends and romantic relationships created spurious results, insofar as teens who adopted gender inconsistent behaviours may have been more likely to bring their romantic partner to the observation session. In addition, the absence of a comparison group composed of opposite-gender friendships prevents definitive conclusions that sex-typed behaviour differences were due to the type of relationship rather than the gender composition. Along the same lines, we were not able to explore whether individual differences in dating experience or emotional well-being had an impact on adolescents' conflict behaviours. Finally, we note some limitations due to the coding of a selected set of conflict behaviours, many of which were low in frequency. A coding scheme assessing a broader range of common conflict strategies would be a useful direction for future research.

CONCLUSION

Despite these limitations, this research extends our understanding of adolescents' management of romantic conflict. Highlighting the presence of gender atypical behaviours in their conflict strategies with romantic partners compared to friends, this study offers new insights into the dynamics of their budding relationships.

Further research into these gendered patterns of interaction will increase our understanding of the dynamics of romantic relationships as adolescents transition into adulthood.

REFERENCES

Adams, R., & Laursen, B. (2001). The organization and dynamics of adolescent conflict with parents and friends. *Journal of Marriage and Family, 63*, 97–110. doi:10.1111/j.1741-3737.2001.00097.x

Brendgen, M., Markiewicz, D., Doyle, A. B., & Bukowski, W. M. (2001). The relations between friendship quality, ranked-friendship preference, and adolescents' behavior with their friends. *Merrill-Palmer Quarterly, 47*, 395–415. doi:10.1353/mpq.2001.0013

Campbell, L., Martin, R. A., & Ward, J. R. (2008). An observational study of humor use while resolving conflict in dating couples. *Personal Relationships, 15*, 41–55. doi:10.1111/j.1475-6811.2007.00183.x

Connolly, J., Craig, W., Goldberg, A., & Pepler, D. (2004). Mixed-gender groups, dating, and romantic relationships in early adolescence. *Journal of Research on Adolescence, 14*, 185–207. doi:10.1111/j.1532-7795.2004.01402003.x

Connolly, J., Furman, W., & Konarski, R. (2000). The role of peers in the emergence of heterosexual romantic relationships in adolescence. *Child Development, 71*, 1395–1408. doi:10.1111/1467-8624.00235

Connolly, J., & McIsaac, C. (2011). *Romantic relationships in adolescence. Social development: Relationships in infancy, childhood, and adolescence* (pp. 180–203). New York, NY: Guilford Press.

Creasey, G., & Hesson-McInnis, M. (2001). Affective responses, cognitive appraisals, and conflict tactics in late adolescent romantic relationships: Associations with attachment orientations. *Journal of Counseling Psychology, 48*, 85–96. doi:10.1037/0022-0167.48.1.85

Dishion, T. J., Crosby, L., Rusby, J. C., Shane, D., Patterson, G. R., & Baker, J. (1989). Peer Process Code: Multidimensional system for observing adolescent peer interactions. Retrieved from the Oregon Social Learning Center, 160 E. 4th Ave., Eugene, OR 97401.

Driver, J. L., & Gottman, J. M. (2004). Daily marital interactions and positive affect during marital conflict among newlywed couples. *Family Process, 43*, 301–314. doi:10.1111/j.1545-5300.2004.00024.x

Furman, W., & Rose, A. J. (2015). Friendships, romantic relationships, and peer relationships. In *Handbook of child psychology and developmental science, vol. 3: Socioemotional processes* (7th ed.), (pp. 932–974). Hoboken, NJ: John Wiley.

Furman, W., & Shomaker, L. B. (2008). Patterns of interaction in adolescent romantic relationships: Distinct features and links to other close relationships. *Journal of Adolescence, 31*, 771–788. doi:10.1016/j.adolescence.2007.10.007

Galliher, R. V., Welsh, D. P., Rostosky, S. S., & Kawaguchi, M. C. (2004). Interaction and relationship quality in late adolescent romantic couples. *Journal of Social and Personal Relationships, 21*, 203–216. doi:10.1177/0265407504041383

Giordano, P. C., Longmore, M. A., & Manning, W. D. (2006). Gender and the meanings of adolescent romantic relationships: A focus on boys. *American Sociological Review, 71*, 260–287. doi:10.1177/000312240607100205

Gottman, J. M. (1994). *What predicts divorce? The relationship between marital processes and marital outcomes.* Hillsdale, NJ: Lawrence Erlbaum Associates.

Ha, T., Dishion, T. J., Overbeek, G., Burk, W. J., & Engels, R. C. (2014). The blues of adolescent romance: Observed affective interactions in adolescent romantic relationships associated with depressive symptoms. *Journal of Abnormal Child Psychology*, *42*, 551–562. doi:10.1007/s10802-013-9808-y

Ha, T., Overbeek, G., Lichtwarck-Aschoff, A., & Engels, R. C. (2013). Do conflict resolution and recovery predict the survival of adolescents' romantic relationships? *PloS ONE*, *8*, e61871. doi:10.1371/journal.pone.0061871

Hill, C. T., & Peplau, L. A. (1998). Premarital predictors of relationship outcomes: A 15 year follow-up of the Boston couples study. In T. N. Bradbury (Ed.), *The developmental course of marital dysfunction* (pp. 237–278). New York, NY: Cambridge University Press.

Jensen-Campbell, L. A., Graziano, W. G., & Hair, E. C. (1996). Personality and relationships as moderators of interpersonal conflict in adolescence. *Merrill-Palmer Quarterly*, *42*, 148–164.

Jones, S., Carrere, S., & Gottman, J. M. (2005). Specific Affect Coding System. In V. Manusov (Ed.), *The sourcebook of nonverbal measures: Going beyond words* (pp. 163–171). Mahwah, NJ: Lawrence Erlbaum Associates.

Keener, E., Strough, J., & DiDonato, L. (2012). Gender differences and similarities in strategies for managing conflict with friends and romantic partners. *Sex Roles*, *67*, 83–97. doi:10.1007/s11199-012-0131-9

Keltner, D., Capps, L., Kring, A. M., Young, R. C., & Heerey, E. A. (2001). Just teasing: A conceptual analysis and empirical review. *Psychological Bulletin*, *127*, 229–248. doi:10.1037/0033-2909.127.2.229

Knox, D. (1971). *Marriage happiness*. Champaign, IL: Research Press.

Laursen, B. (1993). Conflict management among close friends. In B. Laursen (Ed.), *Close friendships in adolescence: New directions for child development* (pp. 39–54). San Francisco, CA: Jossey-Bass.

Laursen, B., Finkelstein, B., & Betts, N. T. (2001). A developmental meta-analysis of peer conflict resolution. *Developmental Review*, *21*, 423–449. doi:10.1006/drev.2000.0531

Laursen, B., & Jensen-Campbell, L. A. (1999). The nature and functions of social exchange in adolescent romantic relationships. In W. Furman, B. B. Brown, & C. Feiring (Eds.), *The development of romantic relationships in adolescence* (pp. 50–74). New York, NY: Cambridge University Press.

Laursen, B., & Williams, V. A. (1997). Perceptions of interdependence and closeness in family and peer relationships among adolescents with and without romantic partners. *New Directions for Child and Adolescent Development*, *1997*, 3–20. doi:10.1002/cd.23219977803

Maccoby, E. E. (1990). Gender and relationships: A developmental account. *American Psychologist*, *45*, 513–520. doi:10.1037/0003-066X.45.4.513

Maccoby, E. E. (1998). *The two sexes: Growing up apart, coming together*. Cambridge: The Belknap Press of Harvard University Press.

Maccoby, E. E. (2002). Gender and social exchange: A developmental perspective. In W. G. Graziano & B. Laursen (Eds.), *Social exchange in development: New directions for child and adolescent development* (pp. 87–105). San Francisco, CA: Jossey-Bass.

Mooney, A., Creeser, R., & Blatchford, P. (1991). Children's view on teasing and fighting in junior schools. *Educational Research*, *33*, 103–112. doi:10.1080/0013188910330203

Multon, K. D. (2010). Interrater reliability. In N. Salkind (Ed.), *Encyclopedia of research design* (pp. 626–628). Thousand Oaks, CA: Sage.

Pellegrini, A. D. (2003). Perceptions and functions of play and real fighting in early adolescence. *Child Development*, *74*, 1522–1533. doi:10.1111/1467-8624.00620

Rose, A. J., & Rudolph, K. D. (2006). A review of sex differences in peer relationship processes: Potential trade-offs for the emotional and behavioral development of girls and boys. *Psychological bulletin*, *132*, 98–131. doi:10.1037/0033-2909.132.1.98

Shulman, S., & Laursen, B. (2002). Adolescent perceptions of conflict in interdependent and disengaged friendships. *Journal of Research on Adolescence, 12*, 353–372. doi:10.1111/1532-7795.00037

Shulman, S., Tuval-Mashiach, R., Levran, E., & Anbar, S. (2006). Conflict resolution patterns and longevity of adolescent romantic couples: A 2-year follow-up study. *Journal of Adolescence, 29*, 575–588. doi:10.1016/j.adolescence.2005.08.018

Shute, R., & Charlton, K. (2006). Anger or compromise? Adolescents' conflict resolution strategies in relation to gender and type of peer relationship. *International Journal of Adolescence and Youth, 13*, 55–69. doi:10.1080/02673843.2006.9747966

Simon, V. A., & Furman, W. (2010). Interparental conflict and adolescents' romantic relationship conflict. *Journal of Research on Adolescence, 20*, 188–209. doi:10.1111/j.1532-7795.2009.00635.x

Suh, E. J., Moskowitz, D. S., Fournier, M. A., & Zuroff, D. C. (2004). Gender and relationships: Influences on agentic and communal behaviors. *Personal Relationships, 11*, 41–60. doi:10.1111/j.1475-6811.2004.00070.x

Underwood, M. K., & Rosen, L. H. (2009). Gender, peer relations, and challenges for girlfriends and boyfriends coming together in adolescence. *Psychology of Women Quarterly, 33*, 16–20. doi:10.1111/j.1471-6402.2008.01468.x

Welsh, D. P., & Shulman, S. (2008). Directly observed interaction within adolescent romantic relationships: What have we learned? *Journal of adolescence, 31*, 877–891. doi:10.1016/j.adolescence.2008.10.001

I get by with a little help from my friends: Examining the peer context of satisfaction with casual sexual relationships and experiences

Haylee K. DeLuca, Shannon E. Claxton, Elizabeth A. Baker, and Manfred H.M. van Dulmen

Department of Psychology, Kent State University, Kent, OH, USA

We examined the role of peers in understanding satisfaction with casual sexual relationships and experiences (CSREs) in young adulthood. Specifically, we examined how perception of peer CSRE engagement, communication with peers about CSREs and peer approval of CSRE engagement were associated with satisfaction both immediately following CSRE engagement and one month after the CSRE occurred. Participants from non-college and college samples completed an online battery of questionnaires at two time points surrounding a high alcohol-consumption event in the USA: Halloween. Path analysis results indicated that peer approval was positively associated with later satisfaction, but only for those in college. Additionally, intentions to communicate with peers were positively associated with satisfaction a month following CSRE, but only for those who engaged in non-penetrative sex. None of the tested associations was qualified by gender.

Peers provide an important context for initiating and maintaining romantic relationships during adolescence and emerging adulthood (Collins, Welsh, & Furman, 2009). Additionally, peers have been linked to attitudes about, and behaviour in, uncommitted sexual relationships and experiences (e.g., Holman & Sillars, 2012). While research suggests peers impact casual sex attitudes and behaviour, less is known about how peers shape individual reactions to these

No potential conflict of interest was reported by the author(s).

encounters. Understanding how the larger social context of one's peer network impacts reactions towards casual sexual relationships and experiences (CSREs) is an important consideration for enhancing empirical research regarding these encounters. Thus, the current paper investigates how various aspects of peer relationships affect feelings about sexual encounters both concurrently and prospectively.

PEER INFLUENCES ON ROMANTIC AND SEXUAL RELATIONSHIPS

For several decades, developmental scientists have acknowledged the importance of non-romantic peer relationships in the development of romantic relationships from early adolescence into adulthood. In adolescence, large, other-gender peer networks are associated with having a romantic relationship, as these contexts allow individuals to interact with other-gender peers (Connolly et al., 2014). However, peers do more than create a venue through which individuals meet potential partners. Close friends provide a working model of relationships, unique from parent–child relationships, that allows adolescents and young adults the opportunity to navigate emotional experiences in voluntary relationships (Connolly, Craig, Goldberg, & Pepler, 2004). Close friends can also offer support for initiating and maintaining romantic relationships, which contributes to the quality of later romantic relationships (Connolly et al., 2004).

However, adolescents and young adults also engage in relationships and experiences that occur outside the context of committed romantic relationships. Many young adults engage in some form of a casual sexual relationship or experience (Garcia & Reiber, 2008). For instance, over 50% of emerging adults report engaging in at least one type of casual sexual relationship or experience (Lambert, Kahn, & Apple, 2003; Paul, McManus, & Hayes, 2000). The term *casual sexual relationships and experiences*, or CSREs (Claxton & van Dulmen, 2013), can be used to denote relationships, as well as experiences, that involve sexual overtones or behaviour but do not occur within the context of 'traditional' ongoing dating relationships. Many individuals report positive reactions to CSREs, such as feeling desirable and happy (Fielder & Carey, 2010), particularly when the encounter involves interest or attraction to the partner (Paul & Hayes, 2002). Despite potential positive outcomes, many college students report feelings of regret after a CSRE (Bachtel, 2013; Fisher, Worth, Garcia, & Meredith, 2012), negative mental health outcomes, such as depression (Fielder, Walsh, Carey, & Carey, 2014; Grello, Welsh, & Harper, 2006), and negative social repercussions (Bachtel, 2013). Additionally, CSREs, similar to any relationship including sexual behaviour, involve a risk for sexually transmitted infections (e.g., Manning, Longmore, & Giordano, 2005).

Given the potential negative consequences of CSREs, it is important to examine other situational components, such as the peer context of these encounters, which may shed light on individual reactions to CSREs. Social Norm Theory (Cialdini, Reno, & Kallgren, 1990) posits that social factors have a profound influence on individual behaviour. Specifically, this theory suggests that two types of social norms particularly affect behaviour: descriptive and injunctive norms. Cialdini et al. (1990) define descriptive norms as the perception of the frequency or prevalence of a behaviour. In contrast, injunctive norms refer to the perception of the approval of a behaviour by others. Both the injunctive and descriptive norms are uniquely associated with sexual behaviour (see van de Bongardt, Reits, Sandfort, & Deković, 2014, for review). They are often established through observation of others, but they can also be formed through explicit communication. In fact, communication about a given behaviour promotes the overestimation of these norms (Lapinski & Rimal, 2005). College students in particular overestimate both injunctive and descriptive norms about sexual behaviour (Barriger & Vélez-Blasini, 2013; Lambert et al., 2003). This overestimation is partially due to direct communication with peers (Lapinski & Rimal, 2005). Thus, the descriptive norm, injunctive norm and communication about a behaviour are three distinct, but related facets of social influence on behaviour. The current paper focuses on the role of these three peer factors as predictors of satisfaction following a CSRE.

The role of peers in CSRES

Perceptions of peer CSRE engagement. Perceptions of peer involvement in sexual behaviour form the descriptive norm (Fielder & Carey, 2010). These descriptive norms regarding peer sexual behaviour are associated with individual sexual activity. For instance, the perception of higher levels of peer sexual activity is associated with having sex in the past month and having more sexual partners (Page, Hammermeister, & Scanlan, 2000). These findings extend to CSRE engagement as well. For example, individuals who report that their friends engaged in a hookup involving penetrative sex are likely to self-report engaging in a penetrative hookup (Berntson, Hoffman, & Luff, 2014). Likewise, individuals who report that their friends have engaged in a friends with benefits relationship (FWB, a non-romantic, sexual relationship between friends) are more likely to report engaging in a FWB relationship themselves (Berntson et al., 2014). While it is clear from these findings that individual perceptions of peer behaviour impact attitudes and behaviour, less is known about how this normative perception impacts reactions to a CSRE. For instance, it is possible that perceptions also impact one's satisfaction following the encounter.

Peer approval. Beyond individual perceptions of peer behaviour, the expressed approval of CSREs by peers, or the injunctive norm (Fielder & Carey, 2010), has been associated with personal behaviour and attitudes. Generally, peer approval of casual sex is associated with holding more favourable attitudes toward casual sex (Holman & Sillars, 2012) and engaging in uncommitted sexual behaviour (Manning et al., 2005). Peer approval of CSREs is also associated with recurring CSREs, as those with peers who approve of FWB relationships are more likely to continue their FWB relationship (Hughes, Morrison, & Asada, 2005). Conversely, those with peers who disapprove of their FWB relationship are less likely to still be in the FWB relationship later (Hughes et al., 2005). Thus, expressed peer approval has a continuous impact on attitudes and behaviour, as peer approval is positively associated with one's decision to continue a CSRE even after the initial encounter has occurred. Similar to the research on the descriptive norm (peer CSRE engagement), the role of the injunctive norm in individual feelings and interpretations of CSREs is less clear. Indeed, perceptions of peer approval could promote feelings of satisfaction following CSREs.

Communication with peers about CSRE involvement. Communication with peers about CSREs has been examined as a predictor for CSRE engagement, as communication likely promotes overestimation of peer behaviours (i.e., the descriptive norm) (Lambert et al., 2003). Communication can also be the form through which both norms are understood (Lapinski & Rimal, 2005). While not all individuals tell their peers about their CSREs (Hughes et al., 2005), research shows that adolescents and young adults are most comfortable discussing sexual encounters with their close friends (Guzmán et al., 2003). Peer communication is positively linked with favourable attitudes toward casual sexual behaviour, especially when respondents report being close to the peer (Hughes et al., 2005), and toward sexual initiation (Busse, Fishbein, Bleakley, & Hennessy, 2010). Given that communication likely shapes one's perceptions of injunctive and descriptive norms, it is important to consider whether communication after a CSRE continues to influence one's opinions about the CSRE. Thus, communicating about a CSRE may lead to the perception that CSREs are normative and that peers accept this behaviour, which may lead to positive emotional responses after a CSRE. In other words, the concurrent effects of these three peer factors likely affect later reactions to CSREs.

Limitations of existing research. Research has yet to fully explain why some individuals report negative reactions to CSREs and others report positive reactions. Furthermore, it is not clear how this association differs by gender and college status. With regard to gender, men report more satisfaction than women following a CSRE (Herold & Mewhinney, 1993). In some studies, men report fewer depressive symptoms than women, following a CSRE (Grello et al., 2006). However, the mechanism underlying these differences is unclear. We pose that social factors, such as peer approval, perception of peer CSRE engagement and communication with peers about CSREs, help shape how females react to CSREs. Given potential double standards regarding sexual behaviour for males and females (Stinson, 2010), it is possible that communicating with peers about CSREs, believing peers are also engaging in CSREs and receiving approval from peers for having a CSRE may be stronger predictors of satisfaction following a CSRE for females, than males.

In addition to gender differences, it is unclear if CSREs are similar in non-college samples. Indeed, the empirical studies discussed previously primarily use college-only samples. Some researchers suggest that college campuses are specific environments in which CSREs are likely to occur (Bogle, 2007, 2008), or that the college context promotes CSREs (Grello et al., 2006). However, this has yet to be examined (Claxton & van Dulmen, 2013).

The current study

While there is substantial empirical evidence indicating that non-romantic peers play an important role in the development of romantic relationships during adolescence and young adulthood, surprisingly little is known as to whether—or how—peers affect CSREs and feelings about CSREs. Given the association between peer CSRE engagement (descriptive norm), peer approval (injunctive norm), and communication with peers about CSREs and self-reports of CSRE engagement, it is likely that these peer factors continue to impact one's reaction to—and understanding of—the CSRE after it occurs. The aim of the current study is to simultaneously examine the relative impact of peer approval, perception of peer CSRE engagement and communication with peers about CSREs on immediate and short-term satisfaction across females and males as well as college and non-college young adults. Examining the relative impact of these social factors on one's satisfaction following a CSRE will help illuminate the mechanisms underlying positive reactions to a CSRE.

In contrast to most other studies in this area (for an exception see Fielder & Carey, 2010), we examined the immediate (daily-diary) and short-term (one-month longitudinal) associations between these peer factors and reactions to CSREs. We designed a model (Figure 1) incorporating the peer factors positively associated with CSRE engagement in previous research (i.e., peer approval, perception of peer CSRE engagement and communication with peers about CSREs), which are the basis of injunctive and descriptive norms, as well as communication with peers which informs these norms (Fielder & Carey, 2010). Specifically, we hypothesized that all three peer constructs would be positively associated with satisfaction at follow-up. Additionally, we predicted immediate satisfaction to be associated with peer constructs at follow-up, as we expect those more satisfied with their CSRE to be less concerned about the negative repercussions of informing their peers (Guzmán et al., 2003).

We hypothesized that the peer constructs would be associated with each other at both time points (see Figure 1). Thus, our hypothesized model incorporates positive associations within and across time. We examined the proposed model

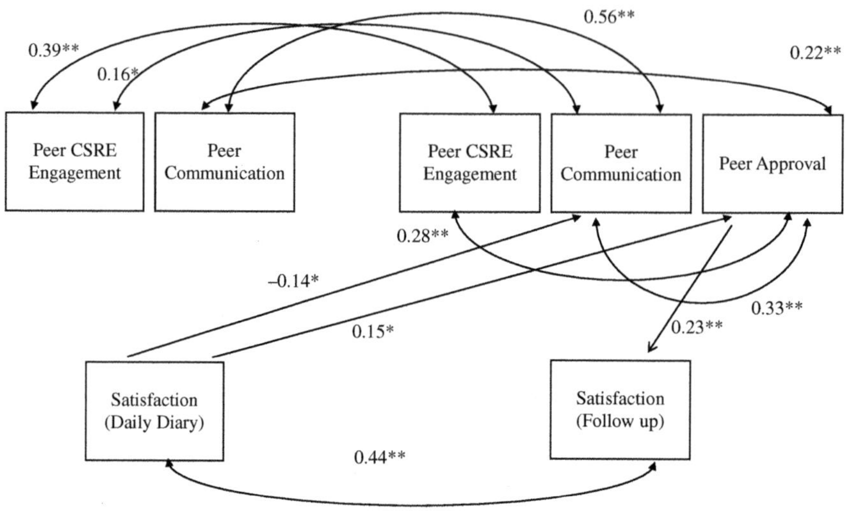

Figure 1. Model results of associations among peer factors and satisfaction following CSRE engagement ($N = 245$). (*Note*: Only statistically significant paths shown ($p < .05$). Values for whole sample are displayed. RMSEA = .08, CFI = .98 for whole sample).

using multi-group analyses to examine gender and sample (college versus non-college) differences.

METHOD

Participants

We utilized data from a larger study approved by the human subjects review board at a Midwestern public university (protocol number: 13-380). The study included two samples: four-year college students from a large Midwestern university (hereafter called "college sample") and a non-college sample from across the USA (hereafter called "non-college sample"). College student participants ($n = 387$) were recruited through the psychology department's subject pool and compensated with course credit. The non-college sample was recruited online through Amazon's Mechanical Turk ($n = 505$) to obtain a sample that was not attending a four-year college or university full-time (92.6% not in school, 4.1% attending part-time, 3.3% attending trade/vocational school or two-year associates college). The non-college sample was monetarily reimbursed $9.50 for completing all assessments in the study. Data were collected over two consecutive years (2013 and 2014), during a high alcohol-consumption event in the USA, Halloween, which occurred during the end of October. Participants were eligible to complete the study if they planned to go out during the Halloween weekend, were between the ages of 18 and 29

(M_{age} College = 19.58, SD = 1.44; M_{age} Non-college = 25.92, SD = 2.62 for those included in analyses), and were currently single (not in a committed dating relationship). The subsample used for the current study ($n = 246$; 177 females, 53 males, 16 unreported; 121 college students) included only individuals who engaged in some form of sexual activity during the Halloween weekend (including kissing, touching, oral sex, sexual intercourse, and/or anal sex). The sample was mostly Caucasian (79%) and heterosexual (82%).

Procedure

The current study uses two waves of data from a larger study. In the first wave, participants completed five days of daily diary assessments that surrounded the Halloween party weekend, which included measures on sexual behaviour, alcohol consumption and affect. Each day, participants completed an online survey reporting on the previous day's alcohol consumption and sexual behaviours. A month later, participants completed an online follow-up assessment (34 participants did not complete the follow-up), which included measures of affect, alcohol consumption and sexual behaviours.

Measures

Sexual behaviour. Sexual behaviour was assessed by asking, "Did you engage in any sexual behaviours (for example, kissing, touching, oral sex, sexual intercourse, anal sex, other) with anyone" on the previous day (see Table 1 for summary of behaviours). Participants also selected the specific behaviours in which they engaged. We included a wide range of behaviours, similar to other researchers (e.g., Barriger & Vélez-Blasini, 2013), because they reflect the spectrum of sexual behaviours in which individuals might engage, and provide a more nuanced understanding of CSRE engagement. Behaviours were coded

TABLE 1
Percentages of sexual behaviour by gender and sample

	Gender		*Sample*		
	Males (%)	*Females (%)*	*College (%)*	*Non-college (%)*	*Total (%)*
Kissing	84.9	92.1	89.4	92.7	91.1
Touching above clothes	73.6	66.7	74.8	61.0	67.9
Touching under clothes	58.5	60.5	61.0	59.3	60.2
Receiving oral sex	37.7	44.1	33.3	48.8	41.1
Giving oral sex	35.8	42.9	49.8	43.9	41.9
Sexual intercourse	52.8	48.6	48.0	52.0	50.0
Anal sex	5.7	7.3	1.6	12.2	6.9
Penetrative sex	52.8	49.7	48.0	53.7	50.8

for CSRE engagement (dichotomous) and penetrative behaviours (vaginal intercourse and anal sex).

Peer sexual behaviour. Perception of peer CSRE engagement was measured at both the daily-diary and follow-up assessments. For the daily-diary assessment, participants responded to one item: "Most of my friends engaged in sexual encounters yesterday." For the follow-up assessment, participants responded to a similar item: "Most of my friends engaged in sexual encounters during the period" (dates were included). Response options ranged from 1 (strongly disagree) to 5 (strongly agree). For our analyses, the highest score across days was used from the daily-diary responses in order reflect those who believed their peers had sex on at least one day.

Peer communication. Peer communication was measured at both the daily-diary and follow-up assessments. In the daily-diary assessment, participants responded to one item: "I plan to tell my friends about the sexual encounter." At the follow-up, participants responded to a similar item: "I told my friends about the sexual encounter I had during Halloween weekend" (dates were included). Response options ranged from 1 (strongly disagree) to 5 (strongly agree). The analyses used highest score from the five daily-diary assessments in order reflect those who were willing to tell their peers about at least one encounter.

Peer approval. Peer approval was measured during the follow-up assessment. Participants responded to one item: "My friends approved of my sexual encounter over that time period." Response options ranged from 1 (strongly disagree) to 5 (strongly agree).

Satisfaction with CSRE. Satisfaction with the CSRE was assessed through two items at both the daily-diary and follow-up assessments: "I enjoyed this experience" and "I am happy that I engaged in this encounter." Response options for these items ranged from 1 (strongly disagree) to 5 (strongly agree) and these two items were averaged to create satisfaction scores ($\alpha = .82-.90$).

ANALYSIS PLAN

We conducted a series of path analyses in Mplus 7.11 (Muthén & Muthén, 2012) to examine the effects of peer approval, perception of peer CSRE engagement and communication with peers about CSREs on satisfaction after CSRE engagement. Path analysis is a special case of structural equation modelling (SEM) that represents a series of interrelated hypotheses in a model using manifest variables. The hypothesized model for the current study included across time associations of satisfaction, peer CSRE engagement and peer communication, as well as paths from peer variables predicting CSRE satisfaction at both time points. Path analysis controls for the shared variance between predictor variables and provides a more conservative test than regression for the hypothesized relationships. We evaluated our model fit using the Confirmatory Fit Index (CFI) and the confidence interval for the root mean squared error of approximation (RMSEA), with CFI values greater than .95 and RMSEA approximation (RMSEA)1, with CFI values greater than .95 and RMSEA CIs near zero suggesting reasonable fit (Hu & Bentler, 1999; Kenny, Kaniskan, & McCoach, 2014). We also examined the χ^2 goodness of fit test, for which a non-significant χ^2 suggests the predicted covariance matrix does not differ significantly from the observed covariance matrix (and thus indicating the model fits the data well). Finally, we tested for group differences (e.g., gender, sample, and sexual behaviours) by applying equality constraints to all paths sequentially. Differences in path coefficients were evaluated using change in χ^2 value, with significant ($p < .05$) change in χ^2 indicating that the two path coefficients differed significantly. All missing data were estimated using the full information maximum likelihood.

RESULTS

Bivariate associations

Frist, we examined the bivariate associations for all variables under study with cohort, gender and sample. There were no statistically significant differences between the cohorts from October 2013 and October 2014 on any of the variables. Chi-square analyses did reveal a statistically significant difference in CSRE engagement for gender [$\chi^2(1) = 8.64$, $p = .003$; females 38%, males 29%] and sample [$\chi^2(1) = 9.92$, $p = .002$; college 34%, non-college 24%]. Statistically significant differences were found between males and females for communication with peers at daily diary [$t(199) = -2.05$, $p = 0.04$] such that females reported more intention to tell peers about the CSRE than males. The college sample reported significantly lower immediate (daily diary) satisfaction [$t(212) = -4.24$, $p < .001$], and follow-up satisfaction [$t(209) = -5.25$, $p = 0.001$] than the non-college sample. The college and non-college samples also differed in communication with peers at daily diary $t(212) = 2.51$, $p = 0.01$ and follow-up [$t(209) = 4.77$, $p < 0.001$], such that the college sample reported more intentions to tell their friends about the CSRE, as well as actually telling their friends about the CSRE. The bivariate associations for the variables included in the analyses are shown in Table 2. These were consistent with the path analysis findings, and are discussed more in depth below.

Association between peer factors and satisfaction

The proposed model fit the data reasonably well, $\chi^2(3) = 7.61$, $p = .05$; CFI = .98, RMSEA 90% CI [0.00–0.15]. All statistically significant ($p < .05$)

TABLE 2
Associations of peer influence and satisfaction after sexual encounter

	1	*2*	*3*	*4*	*5*	*6*	*7*
1. Peer CSRE engagement (daily diary)	–						
2. Peer communication (daily diary)	.11	–					
3. Peer CSRE engagement (follow-up)	.39**	.11	–				
4. Peer communication (follow-up)	.12	.52**	.17*	–			
5. Peer approval (follow-up)	.21**	.30**	.39**	.47**	–		
6. Satisfaction after CSRE (daily diary)	.04	.14*	.02	− .02	.21**	–	
7. Satisfaction after CSRE (follow-up)	.11	.04	.13	− .05	.27**	.47*	–

Notes: **= $p < .01$, *= $p < .05$

paths are depicted in Figure 1. As hypothesized, peer approval predicted satisfaction at follow-up ($\beta = .23$, $p = .002$). Additionally, satisfaction immediately following CSRE was positively associated with peer approval at follow-up ($\beta = .15$, $p = .02$). However, contrary to our hypothesis, satisfaction immediately following CSRE was negatively associated with communicating with peers at follow-up ($\beta = -.14$, $p = .03$). Though not a central hypothesis, several peer variables were significantly associated across and within time, and satisfaction was significantly associated across time.

Association between peer factors and satisfaction: Gender differences

Given that previous research has shown gender differences in reactions to CSREs (e.g., Grello et al., 2006), we examined gender differences in the model by running multi-group models in Mplus, and applying equality constraints. However, all paths in this model could be constrained to be equal for males and females, suggesting that males and females are not showing statistically significant differences in the associations between these variables.

Association between peer factors and satisfaction: College and non-college

As some scholars have argued that CSREs occur on college campuses and traditional dating is more likely to occur after college (Bogle, 2007, 2008), we examined sample differences in the model by again conducting a multi-group model in Mplus and applying equality constraints. All paths, except the path from peer approval to follow up satisfaction, could be constrained to be equal. This suggests that the impact of peer approval on satisfaction a month after CSRE differs significantly between our college and non-college samples, such that the association between peer approval and short-term satisfaction is stronger for the college sample ($\beta = .45$, $p < .001$), as compared to the non-college sample ($\beta = -.10$, $p = .36$).

Additionally, due to the differences in age between the two samples, we reran this multi-group model, controlling for age. Controlling for age did not alter any of the significant paths observed, although age predicted immediate ($\beta = .06$, $p < .001$) and short-term satisfaction ($\beta = .06$, $p < .001$).

Additional analyses: Sexual behaviours

Given the potential differences in reactions to penetrative and non-penetrative CSREs (Fielder & Carey, 2010), we examined the differences between those who engaged in penetrative versus non-penetrative sexual behaviours by running a multi-group model. We examined difference by applying equality constraints and examining the change in χ^2 value. Results indicated associations between immediate perceptions of peer CSRE and follow-up approval, and immediate perceptions of peer CSRE and follow-up perceptions of peer CSRE could not be constrained to be equal, as these associations were stronger for those who engaged in non-penetrative sexual behaviours. Additionally, the association between intentions to communicate with peers and follow-up satisfaction could not be constrained to be equal, such that peer communication intentions are more strongly associated with satisfaction a month after CSRE for those who engaged in non-penetrative sex ($\beta = .25$, $p = .04$) compared to those who engaged in penetrative sex ($\beta = -.17$, $p = .09$).

DISCUSSION

Our study provides an important contribution to the literature, as it suggests that normative influence may have an impact on satisfaction following a CSRE. Overall, our results show few significant differences between males and females, college and non-college individuals, and those who engage in penetrative and non-penetrative behaviours. More specifically, the only significant difference found based on college status was that peer approval was more strongly associated with satisfaction a month following CSRE for college students than non-college students. In other words, individual satisfaction is more affected by peer approval when one is immersed in a four-year college setting. Moreover, for those who engaged in non-penetrative sex, intentions to communicate with peers were more strongly associated with satisfaction a month later, as compared to those who engaged in penetrative sexual behaviours.

In general, our results suggest that the injunctive norm, but not the descriptive norm or communication, has an impact on satisfaction following CSREs, for college students. College students are likely more influenced by peer approval due to their environment, which surrounds them with their peers on a daily basis. In contrast, our non-college sample may be less enmeshed with their peer group. Additionally, research has shown that the effects of peer influence on risky decision-making decrease with age (e.g., Gardner & Steinberg, 2005), so these differences may also be explained by the age or maturity of the non-college sample. Thus, even though our non-college and college samples report similar levels of peer CSRE engagement and peer approval, the non-college sample does not appear as affected by this normative influence.

Limitations

While our results represent an important contribution to the literature on CSRE engagement, our findings should be interpreted with caution in light of potential limitations. First, we had a limited sample of males, and thus the small differences in likelihood of engaging in a CSRE should be interpreted with caution. Moreover, our findings suggest that for males and females, peers play a similar role in satisfaction following a CSRE.

Additionally, we acknowledge that our constructs were limited. Future research would benefit from more nuanced measures of peer influence, such as examining influences of close friendships and peer relationships, because sexual activity has been shown to be more strongly associated with behaviour of close friends than peers (e.g., van de Bongardt et al., 2014). Similarly, our satisfaction construct consisted of two items. While—to our knowledge—this is the first study to longitudinally investigate the role of multiple aspects of peer relationships in predicting satisfaction with CSREs, future research should simultaneously examine aspects of satisfaction and dissatisfaction following CSREs to determine the social factors that predict each reaction. Additionally, though we did examine two sexual behaviours (penetrative and non-penetrative), future research should continue to investigate how specific behaviours and partner characteristics differentially predict satisfaction for males and females, and college and non-college individuals.

CONCLUSIONS

In conclusion, our findings suggest that injunctive normative influences are a stronger predictor of satisfaction for those enmeshed in a four-year college or university campus, indicating that the four-year college campus environment plays a role in reactions to CSREs. Therefore, social and contextual factors should be considered when examining individuals' reactions to CSREs. Additionally, our work shows that an important contextual factor may be the behaviours involved in a given CSRE, as certain sexual behaviours—but not others—affect the impact of these normative beliefs on satisfaction with CSRE. Future theory and research should incorporate these social and contextual factors to develop a comprehensive theory for CSRE engagement in both college and non-college environments.

REFERENCES

Bachtel, M. K. (2013). Do hookups hurt? Exploring college students' experiences and perceptions. *Journal of Midwifery & Women's Health, 58*, 41–48. doi:10.1111/j.1542-2011.2012.00266.x

Barriger, M., & Vélez-Blasini, C. J. (2013). Descriptive and injunctive social norm overestimation in hooking up and their role as predictors of hook-up activity in a college student sample. *Journal of sex research, 50*, 84–94. doi:10.1080/00224499.2011.607928

Berntson, M. A., Hoffman, K. L., & Luff, T. L. (2014). College as context: Influences on interpersonal sexual scripts. *Sexuality & Culture, 18*, 149–165. doi:10.1007/s12119-013-9180-7

Bogle, K. A. (2007). The shift from dating to hooking up in college: What scholars have missed. *Sociology Compass, 1*, 775–788. doi:10.1111/j.1751-9020.2007.00031.x

Bogle, K. A. (2008). *Hooking up: Sex, dating, and relationships on campus.* New York, NY: New York University Press.

Busse, P., Fishbein, M., Bleakley, A., & Hennessy, M. (2010). The role of communication with friends in sexual initiation. *Communication Research, 37*, 239–255. doi:10.1177/0093650209356393

Cialdini, R. B., Reno, R. R., & Kallgren, C. A. (1990). A focus theory of normative conduct: Recycling the concept of norms to reduce littering in public places. *Journal of Personality and Social Psychology, 58*, 1015–1026. doi:10.1037/0022-3514.58.6.1015

Claxton, S. E., & van Dulmen, M. H. (2013). Casual sexual relationships and experiences in emerging adulthood. *Emerging Adulthood, 1*, 138–150. doi:10.1177/2167696813487181

Collins, W. A., Welsh, D. P., & Furman, W. (2009). Adolescent romantic relationships. *Annual Review of Psychology, 60*, 631–652. doi:10.1146/annurev.psych.60.110707.163459

Connolly, J., Craig, W., Goldberg, A., & Pepler, D. (2004). Mixed-gender groups, dating, and romantic relationships in early adolescence. *Journal of Research on Adolescence, 14*, 185–207.

Connolly, J., McIsaac, C., Shulman, S., Wincentak, K., Joly, L., Heifetz, M., & Bravo, V. (2014). Development of romantic relationships in adolescence and emerging adulthood: Implications for community mental health. *Canadian Journal of Community Mental Health, 33*, 7–19. doi:10.7870/cjcmh-2014-002

Fielder, R. L., & Carey, M. P. (2010). Predictors and consequences of sexual "hookups" among college students: A short-term prospective study. *Archives of Sexual Behavior, 39*, 1105–1119. doi:10.1007/s10508-008-9448-4

Fielder, R. L., Walsh, J. L., Carey, K. B., & Carey, M. P. (2014). Sexual hookups and adverse health outcomes: A longitudinal study of first-year college women. *The Journal of Sex Research, 51*, 131–144. doi:10.1080/00224499.2013.848255

Fisher, M. L., Worth, K., Garcia, J. R., & Meredith, T. (2012). Feelings of regret following uncommitted sexual encounters in Canadian university students. *Culture, Health & Sexuality, 14*, 45–57. doi:10.1080/13691058.2011.619579

Garcia, J. R., & Reiber, C. (2008). Hook-up behavior: A biopsychosocial perspective. *Journal of Social, Evolutionary, and Cultural Psychology, 2*, 192–208. doi:10.1037/h0099345

Gardner, M., & Steinberg, L. (2005). Peer influence on risk taking, risk preference, and risky decision making in adolescence and adulthood: An experimental study. *Developmental Psychology, 41*, 625–635. doi:10.1037/0012-1649.41.4.625

Grello, C. M., Welsh, D. P., & Harper, M. S. (2006). No strings attached: The nature of casual sex in college students. *Journal of Sex Research, 43*, 255–267. doi:10.1080/00224490609552324

Guzmán, B. L., Schlehofer-Sutton, M. M., Villanueva, C. M., Stritto, M. E. D., Casad, B. J., & Feria, A. (2003). Let's talk about sex: How comfortable discussions about sex impact teen sexual behavior. *Journal of Health Communication, 8*, 583–598.

Herold, E. S., & Mewhinney, D. A. K. (1993). Gender differences in casual sex and AIDS prevention: A survey of dating bars. *Journal of Sex Research, 30*, 36–42. doi:10.1080/00224499309551676

Holman, A., & Sillars, A. (2012). Talk about "hooking up": The influence of college student social networks on nonrelationship sex. *Health Communication, 27*, 205–216. doi:10.1080/10410236.2011.575540

Hu, L. T., & Bentler, P. M. (1999). Cutoff criteria for fit indexes in covariance structure analysis: Conventional criteria versus new alternatives. *Structural Equation Modeling: A Multidisciplinary Journal, 6*(1), 1–55. doi:10.1080/10705519909540118

Hughes, M., Morrison, K., & Asada, K. J. K. (2005). What's love got to do with it? Exploring the impact of maintenance rules, love attitudes, and network support on friends with benefits relationships. *Western Journal of Communication, 69*, 49–66. doi:10.1080/10570310500034154

Kenny, D. A., Kaniskan, B., & McCoach, D. B. (2014). The performance of RMSEA in models with small degrees of freedom. *Sociological Methods & Research*, Advance online publication. doi: 10.1177/0049124114543236

Lambert, T. A., Kahn, A. S., & Apple, K. J. (2003). Pluralistic ignorance and hooking up. *Journal of Sex Research, 40*, 129–133. doi:10.1080/00224490309552174

Lapinski, M. K., & Rimal, R. N. (2005). An explication of social norms. *Communication Theory, 15*, 127–147. doi:10.1111/j.1468-2885.2005.tb00329.x

Manning, W. D., Longmore, M. A., & Giordano, P. C. (2005). Adolescents' involvement in non-romantic sexual activity. *Social Science Research, 34*, 384–407. doi:10.1016/j.ssresearch.2004.03.001

Muthén & Muthén. (1998-2012). *Mplus User's Guide* (Seventh Edition). Los Angeles, CA: Muthén & Muthén.

Page, R. M., Hammermeister, J. J., & Scanlan, A. (2000). Everybody's not doing it: Misperceptions of college students' sexual activity. *American Journal of Health Behavior, 24*, 387–394. doi:10.5993/AJHB.24.5.7

Paul, E. L., & Hayes, K. A. (2002). The casualties of "casual" sex: A qualitative exploration of the phenomenology of college students' hookups. *Journal of Social and Personal Relationships, 19*, 639–661. doi:10.1177/0265407502195006

Paul, E. L., McManus, B., & Hayes, A. (2000). "Hookups": Characteristics and correlates of college students' spontaneous and anonymous sexual experiences. *Journal of Sex Research, 37*, 76–88. doi:10.1080/00224490009552023

Stinson, R. D. (2010). Hooking up in young adulthood: A review of factors influencing the sexual behavior of college students. *Journal of College Student Psychotherapy, 24*, 98–115. doi:10.1080/87568220903558596

Van de Bongardt, D., Reitz, E., Sandfort, T., & Deković, M. (2014). A meta-analysis of the relations between three types of peer norms and adolescent sexual behavior. *Personality and Social Psychology Review*, Advance online publication. doi:1088868314544223

Let's talk openly about sex: Sexual communication, self-esteem and efficacy as correlates of sexual well-being

Shawna Mastro, and Melanie J. Zimmer-Gembeck

School of Applied Psychology and Menzies Health Institute of Queensland, Griffith University, Australia

Drawing from theories of sexual development, the aim of this study was investigate whether sexual well-being was more positive when youth reported more frequent and better quality sex-related communication, and greater sexual subjectivity (sexual body esteem and pleasure self-efficacy). Sexual well-being was measured with reference to partnered behaviour, including safe-sex behavioural competence, sexual assertiveness, and emotional reactions. Young adults ($N = 209$; 61% female) aged 17–21 completed questionnaires. While also considering age, gender, romantic status and coital experience in regression analyses, participants higher in competence reported more frequent communication with mothers in high school, and current higher quality communication with mothers and friends. Participants reported more positive emotions related to sex when they had better quality communication with their friends. Associations of sexual subjectivity with greater sexual well-being were found, and small indirect effects were found between retrospectively reported communication frequency and sexual well-being via pleasure self-efficacy.

Significant advances have been made toward understanding the factors that increase risk for early sexual onset, unprotected sexual behaviour, pregnancy, and sexually transmitted infections among adolescents and young adults (for a review see Byers & Rehman, 2014). However, there has been relative neglect of the parallel research focus essential for defining and understanding the

No potential conflict of interest was reported by the authors.

development of healthy sexuality (Fortenberry, 2014; Harden, 2014). To address this imbalance, there has been an enhanced interest in considering both the positive and negative aspects of youths' sexual experience, such as sexual satisfaction and emotional responses (Zimmer-Gembeck, See, & O'Sullivan, 2015). Investigation of sexual-self perceptions has supported this effort. In particular, research on youth's sexual subjectivity, which has been defined as including sexual body-esteem and perceptions of efficacy and entitlement to desire and pleasure, has aided in an understanding of well-being in this age group (Horne & Zimmer-Gembeck, 2006; Tolman, 2002).

Adolescent sexual developmental theory (e.g., Tolman & McClelland, 2011) and life course views on sexual development (Fortenberry, 2014) are foundations for much of this positively framed research. These theories describe adolescent sexual behaviour as normative, and recognise emerging sexuality as a developmental milestone associated with a range of individual attitudes and beliefs, and social experiences in the family, with peers, and within the wider community. With these theories as a guide, we extended on previous research that has examined romantic interactions and sexual behaviour as correlates of sexual well-being in adolescence and early adulthood (Zimmer-Gembeck, Ducat, & Boislard-Pepin, 2011) by adding a focus on parents and friendship as potential social resources for talking about sex-related topics, and considering how this communication could be associated with *sexual well-being*. Our conceptualisation of sexual well-being aligned with current definitions that include positive affective responses to sexual behaviour (Byers & Rehman, 2014) and reduced negative affective responses (e.g., Harden, 2014; Tolman, 2002). However, we extended the conceptualisation of sexual well-being to include partnered behaviours that reflect sexual competence and protective behaviours (i.e., safe-sex behavioural competence and sexual assertiveness) for a balanced focus on "well-being" and "protective" elements. Thus, sexual well-being was defined as protective sexual behaviours, as well as cognitions and emotions that are associated with sexual behaviour. Together, these aspects of what we refer to here as sexual well-being reflect a range of cognitions, emotions, and behaviours related to partnered sexual interactions, which we argue better reflect well-being and healthy sexual functioning during late adolescence and early adulthood.

In addition, we measured youth's sexual subjectivity in order to assess self-related aspects of sexuality that did not directly depend on sexual behaviour. Sexual subjectivity included sexual body esteem and sexual self-efficacy. Theory has pointed to the unique role of personal factors, including esteem, autonomy and efficacy, as salient to shaping positive life experiences, well-being and positive affect (Pearson, 2006; Zimmer-Gembeck, Ducat, & Collins, 2011). Thus, sexual subjectivity was examined as a personal factor expected to be associated with sexual-well-being.

COMMUNICATION AND SEXUAL WELL-BEING

Parents and peers can be essential sources of information and support during sexual development in adolescence. Yet, communication with parents and peers has not been examined in relation to sexual well-being, and it seems important to examine both past and current sex-related communication as each are potentially important to sexual well-being in young adulthood.

Communication with parents

Conversations about sex with parents provide important information that can guide sexual development, including values and beliefs about sex, and understanding sexual risk and behaviour (Lefkowitz & Espinosa-Hernandez, 2007). In terms of content, young people report discussing a wide range of sexuality-related topics with their parents (Sneed, Somoza, Jones, & Alfaro, 2013), but researchers often focus on general topics of communication, rather than the quality of sex-related communication, and conversation related to behaviour, rather than sex-related cognitions and emotions (Lefkowitz & Espinosa-Hernandez, 2007). However, parents and adolescents often find communication about sex and sexuality difficult (Rosenthal & Feldman, 1999). Parents' concerns about embarrassment, a lack of knowledge and interpersonal skills, and emotions related to sex in general have been found to influence how much they communicate with their adolescents about sex (Guilamo-Ramos, Jaccard, Dittus, & Collins, 2008), and can also affect the quality of such communication (Lefkowitz & Espinosa-Hernandez, 2007). Such findings suggest that the frequency, as well as quality, of sexual communication may be important to consider as correlates of sexual well-being.

Likewise, when parents discuss sex and sexuality, adolescents have reported feeling uncomfortable, suspect their parents of prying into their private affairs, and fear punishment if they are perceived to be sexually active (Guilamo-Ramos et al., 2008; Rosenthal & Feldman, 1999). Thus, young people also sense this variety of comfort and approval and may respond accordingly. Observational studies have indicated that the way in which adolescents communicate with their parents about sex can be problematic. For example, adolescents have been found to prefer parents to provide structure to conversations about sex, as opposed to the autonomy support that young people prefer in other, non-sex related communication with parents (Mauras, Grolnick, & Friendly, 2013). Nevertheless, youth report that they would like their parents to discuss positive aspects of sexuality (Warren, 1995), and retrospective reports have indicated the desire for more information from parents that informs the emotional aspects of sexual behaviour (Hutchinson & Cederbaum, 2011).

Communication with friends

In addition to parents, youth often look to their friends for input about sex and romance (Connolly, Craig, Goldberg, & Pepler, 2004). Researchers have shown that friends serve as models and sources of support for initiating and pursuing romantic relationships, and also for coping with difficulties with them (Fortenberry, 2014). There is a consensus emerging that young people learn more about sex from interactions with their peers, either their romantic partners or same-sex friends, than from any other sources (Fortenberry, 2014; Sprecher, Harris, & Meyers, 2008).

When focused on quality and openness, studies have found that communication about sex with peers is associated with less risky sexual behaviour. For example, Guzmán et al. (2003) found that adolescents' comfort about sex-based discussions with their friends was associated with intentions to delay intercourse, and Halpern-Felsher, Kropp, Boyer, Tschann, and Ellen (2004) found that greater self-efficacy to communicate with peers about sex-related topics was associated with more frequent condom use. However, adolescents who report peers as a main resource of sexual information, as opposed to parents or religious leaders, endorsed beliefs that made it likely to engage in sexual behaviour, and perceived sexual activity as more normative amongst their peers (Bleakley, Hennessy, Fishbein, & Jordan, 2009). There is relatively little research, however, on how sex-related communication with friends is associated with sexual well-being or sexual subjectivity.

THE PRESENT STUDY: COMMUNICATION, SEXUAL SUBJECTIVITY, AND SEXUAL WELL-BEING

In the present study, we investigated whether more frequent sex-related communication in high school, and better quality communication as a young adult, with mother, father and best friend were positively associated with sexual well-being and sexual subjectivity, measured as greater safe-sex behavioural competence, sexual assertiveness, more positive and less negative emotional responses to sexual experiences, sexual esteem and efficacy to achieve pleasure. Two aspects of communication were measured, namely retrospective reports of frequency of sex-related communication in adolescence (i.e., during high school), and current perceived quality of current sex-related communication (i.e., in young adulthood). Measuring sexual communication in these two time frames allowed the results to be integrated with previous research that assessed sex-related communication frequency in adolescence (Guilamo-Ramos et al., 2008; Akers, Holland, & Bost, 2011), but also extended the findings of past research to test whether past frequency and current quality of communication were each associated with sexual well-being and sexual subjectivity. Moreover, our measurement of past frequency of communication gave some temporal ordering to our measures. This ordering allowed us to examine indirect effects between past communication frequency with current sexual well-being via sexual subjectivity.

Communication with parents and friends about sexual issues may not have direct influences on sexual behaviour, but rather they may have indirect influence because communication serves to directly enhance youths' own beliefs about the sexual self, which then underpins their regulation and experiences of their sexual behaviour. Based on theories of adolescent sexual development (Tolman, 2002; Tolman & McClelland, 2011; Zimmer-Gembeck et al., 2011; Zimmer-Gembeck & French, in press), some of these cognitive resources are captured in the notion of sexual subjectivity, which includes feelings of sexual esteem and efficacy to achieve pleasurable and avoid non-pleasurable experiences. It was expected that more frequent communication in high school with mother, father and best friend would be associated with greater sexual well-being, but that there would also be unique associations of sexual subjectivity with greater sexual well-being. Moreover, the inclusion of sexual subjectivity as a correlate of sexual well-being was expected to result in only indirect associations between earlier frequency of communication and sexual well-being, so that communication was expected to be associated with sexual well-being via sexual subjectivity.

Finally, current quality of communication about sex-related topics with mother, father and best friend was also investigated. We expected that quality of communication and sexual subjectivity would be uniquely associated with greater sexual well-being even after accounting for a range of covariates.

METHOD

Participants

Participants were 209 young women (61%) and men (39%) aged 17–21 years ($M = 19.28$, SD = 1.0) who reported some sexual experience (e.g., kissing, touching, oral sex and/or intercourse). Another 39 youth participated but were not included in the analyses because they reported no sexual experience ($n = 17$) and or did not report sexual communication with a mother, father or best friend ($n = 22$). Overall, 79% reported a history of sexual intercourse, 39% reported a current steady romantic relationship, 93% of the participants were white Australian, 82% described themselves as heterosexual, 91% were full time students and 65% lived with a parent or parents.

Procedure

After ethics review committee approval, participants were recruited through a psychology student subject pool, where they received course credit for completing the online survey (66%). Potential participants were also approached in university common areas (e.g., eating areas) to complete the 15-min survey in exchange for a food voucher, and placed their completed survey in a sealed envelope (34%). Participants were provided with information and consent forms prior to survey completion. Some differences between online and hard copy participants were detected. Therefore, the method (0 = hard copy, 1 = online version) was included as a covariate in analyses.

Measures

Frequency of sex-related communication during high school. Frequency of sex-related communication during high school was measured with a subset of items adapted for mother, father and best friend from the Close Friend Communication about Sex Scale (Lefkowitz, Boone, & Shearer, 2004). Participants were asked how much they talked from the age of 13 until they left high school with their mother, father and best friend about eight sex-related issues, such as sexuality and contraception. Responses ranged from *never* (1) to *often* (5). Cronbach's αs for young women and men, respectively, were: mother .90 and .90; father .89 and .86; best friend .88 and .89.

Current quality of sex-related communication. To measure current quality with sex-related communication with mother, father and best friend, eight items from a 13-item Quality of Adolescent Sex-Related Communication scale were utilised (Feldman & Rosenthal, 2000). Items began with, "If my Mother/Father/Best friend discussed sex and sex-related issues with me, I would . . . ". Items asked about comfort and ability to speak freely about sex-related topics (e.g.," . . . share my sexual experiences"). Answers ranged from *strongly disagree* (1) to *strongly agree* (4). Negatively worded items were reverse scored, and items were averaged. Higher scores indicated higher quality communication, and Cronbach's αs for young women and men, respectively, were: mother .92 and .89; father .87 and .92; best friend .88 and .89.

Safe-sex behavioural competence and sexual assertiveness. Safe-sex behavioural competence and sexual assertiveness were measured with items from the Sexual Self-Efficacy Scale (SSES; Rosenthal, Moore, & Flynn, 1991). Four items from the SSES (e.g. "Choose when and with whom to have sex") measured sexual assertiveness, and four items (e.g. Buy condoms/contraceptives") measured safe-sex behavioural competence. Participants reported the certainty performing each behaviour, with responses from *very uncertain* (1) to *very certain* (5). Cronbach's α were .74 and .75 for young women, and .65 and .69 for young men.

Positive/negative emotional responses to sexual experience. Six positive items (e.g., excited) and seven negative items (e.g., exploited) from the First Coital Affective Reaction Scale (Schwartz, 1998) measured emotional responses to sexual experience, in general, with an adaptation that referred to all sexual experiences (e.g., kissing, touching and/or intercourse) with responses from *strongly disagree* (1) to *strongly agree* (5). Cronbach's αs for young women and men, respectively, were: positive emotions .88 and .74; negative emotions .86 and .79.

Sexual subjectivity: Sexual body esteem and sexual self-efficacy. Two subscales from the Female Sexual Subjectivity Inventory (Horne & Zimmer-Gembeck, 2006) were used to measure sexual body-esteem and self-efficacy in achieving sexual pleasure. Five items assessed sexual body-esteem (e.g., "I am not concerned about how I look when naked"), and three items assessed self-efficacy in sexual pleasure achievement (e.g., "If I were to have sex with someone, I'd show my partner what I want"). Items had been shown to be reliable and valid with young men in previous research (Zimmer-Gembeck & French, in press). Response options ranged from *strongly disagree* (1) to *strongly agree* (5). Cronbach's αs for young women and men, respectively, were: sexual body-esteem .81 and .79; sexual self-efficacy .76 and .68.

Overview of analyses

Standard regression analyses were utilised to examine the associations of communication frequency in high school and sexual subjectivity with sexual assertiveness, safe-sex behavioural competence, and positive and negative emotional responses to sexual behaviour. In these models, gender, coital experience and romantic partner status were also examined. Indirect effects were investigated via sexual subjectivity for communication frequency only due to its defined temporal precedence. Bootstrapping (5000 samples) was used to estimate indirect effects and calculate 95% confidence intervals. Similar standard regression analyses were utilised to examine the associations of current communication quality and sexual subjectivity variables with sexual well-being. Indirect effects were not tested in these concurrent models.

RESULTS

Correlations

Correlations between all continuous measures are reported in Table 1. Multiple measures of communication were significantly positively associated with each aspect of sexual well-being, with the exception of negative emotional responses to sex. Moreover, the two measures of sexual subjectivity, sexual body esteem

TABLE 1
Correlations between all primary measures ($N = 209$)

	1	*2*	*3*	*4*	*5*	*6*	*7*	*8*	*9*	*10*	*11*	*12*
1. Past comm freq – Mother	–											
2. Past comm freq – Father	.51**	–										
3. Past comm freq – Friend	.45**	.25**	–									
4. Current comm qual – Mother	.57**	.35**	.24**	–								
5. Current comm qual – Father	.12	.53**	.00	.50**	–							
6. Current comm qual – Friend	.18**	.07	.36**	.16*	−.02	–						
7. Sexual body esteem	−.07	.06	.05	.06	.18**	.03	–					
8. Pleasure self-efficacy	.14*	.21**	.20**	.11	.11	.15*	.21**	–				
9. Sexual assertiveness	.19**	.07	.05	.15*	−.03	.16*	.03	.19**	–			
10. Safe-sex competence	.27**	.21**	.21**	.28**	.16*	.25**	.21**	.22**	.50**	–		
11. Pos emotional responses	−.01	.13[a]	.05	.03	.16*	.14*	.33**	.34**	.11	.16*	–	
12. Neg emotional responses	.09	−.02	.10	.03	−.06	−.11	−.38**	−.23**	−.14*	−.17*	−.32**	–
13. Age	.15*	.13	.20*	.17*	.08	−.01	.05	.06	.07	.16*	−.03	−.01
M	2.16	1.58	3.48	2.09	1.82	3.25	3.16	3.74	4.29	4.06	4.04	2.61
SD	.91	.67	.93	.65	.68	.48	.69	.60	.63	.67	.67	.79

Notes: Comm = communication. Freq = frequency. Qual = quality. Pos = positive. Neg = Negative.
[a]$p = .06$. *$p < .05$. **$p < .01$.

and pleasure self-efficacy, were significantly associated with most measures of sexual well-being, including more safe-sex competence, and more positive responses and fewer negative responses to sexual behaviour. Only pleasure self-efficacy was significantly associated with assertiveness. Finally, communication was significantly associated with heightened sexual body esteem and pleasure self-efficacy, with more numerous associations between communication and pleasure self-efficacy than between communication and sexual body esteem.

Past communication frequency, sexual subjectivity and sexual well-being

Sexual assertiveness and safe-sex behaviour competence. Table 2 shows the results of regressing sexual assertiveness and safe-sex behavioural competence on all measures. For sexual assertiveness, young women, those with no coital experience, those with current partners, and those higher in one sexual subjectivity scale, pleasure self-efficacy, reported being more assertive. All indirect effects via sexual body esteem were not significant (see Table 3). Small, indirect effects between father and friend communication frequency and sexual assertiveness via pleasure self-efficacy were significant (see Table 4).

For safe-sex behaviour competence, greater communication frequency with mother and greater sexual body esteem were associated with more competence. There was a small but significant indirect effect between communication frequency with mother and safe-sex competence via sexual body esteem (see Table 3), and significant indirect effects between father and friend communication frequency and safe-sex behaviour competence via pleasure self-efficacy (see Table 4).

Emotional responses to sexual experience. In the models of positive and negative responses to sexual experiences, young adults with greater sexual body-esteem and sexual self-efficacy reported more positive and less negative responses to sex (see Table 2). Indirect effects via sexual body esteem were not significant (see Table 3). Significant (small) indirect effects were found for positive responses, where the association between mother, father and friend communication frequency and positive responses was indirect via pleasure self-efficacy (see Table 4).

Current communication quality, sexual subjectivity and sexual well-being

Sexual assertiveness and safe-sex behaviour competence. For communication quality and sexual assertiveness, young women, those reporting current steady romantic relationships, those with no coital experience, and those higher in

TABLE 2
Results of regressing safe-sex behavioural competence and sexual assertiveness on communication frequency and sexual subjectivity ($N = 209$)

	Sexual assertiveness		*Safe-sex competence*		*Positive emotional responses*		*Negative emotional responses*	
Independent variables	B (*SE*)	β	B (*SE*)	β	B (*SE*)	β	B (*SE*)	β
Version	−.02 (.82)	−.01	−.15 (.11)	−.11	−.17 (.11)	−.12	.06 (.13)	.04
Gender	.39 (.13)	.31**	−.04 (.14)	−.03	.08 (.13)	.06	.18 (.16)	.11
Age	.05 (.04)	.07	.06 (.04)	.10	−.04 (.04)	−.06	−.01 (.05)	−.01
Relationship status	.23 (.09)	.18*	.16 (.10)	.12	.15 (.10)	.11	−.09 (.12)	−.05
Coital Experience	−.30 (.13)	−.17*	−.10 (.14)	−.05	.24 (.13)	.12	−.19 (.16)	−.08
Comm freq – Mother	.03 (.07)	.04	.16 (.07)	.22*	−.07 (.07)	−.09	−.02 (.08)	−.03
Comm freq – Father	.06 (.08)	.07	.00 (.09)	.00	.12 (.09)	.12	.05 (.10)	.04
Comm freq – Friend	−.07 (.05)	−.11	.07 (.06)	.10	.01 (.05)	.02	.10 (.07)	.11
Sexual body esteem	.04 (.06)	.04	.16 (.07)	.16*	.21 (.06)	.22**	−.35 (.08)	−.31***
Pleasure self-efficacy	.21 (.07)	.20**	.11 (.08)	.10	.28 (.07)	.25***	−.22 (.09)	−.16*

Notes: Model 1: $F(10, 198) = 4.56$, $p < .001$, $R^2 = .19$; Model 2: $F(10, 198) = 4.18$, $p < .001$, $R^2 = .17$; Model 3: $F(10, 198) = 6.19$, $p < .001$, $R^2 = .24$; Model 4: $F(10, 198) = 5.32$, $p < .001$, $R^2 = .21$. Comm = Communication; Freq = frequency; Gender: 0 = males, 1 = females. Version: 0 = hard copy, 1 = online version. Relationship status: 0 = No partner, 1 = Current steady partner. Coital experience: 0 = No, 1 = Yes.
$^*p < .05$. $^{**}p < .01$. $^{***}p < .001$.

TABLE 3

Path estimates, standard errors and confidence intervals for models mediated by sexual body esteem ($N = 209$)

	Unstandardised				Standardised			
Models	*a × b effect*	*SE*	*Lower 95% CI*	*Upper 95% CI*	*a × b effect*	*SE*	*Lower 95% CI*	*Upper 95% CI*
1. Comm Freq – Mother → Sexual Assertiveness	−.003	.011	−.038	.012	−.002	.007	−.025	.008
2. Comm Freq – Mother → Safe-sex Competence	−.037*	.024	−.100	−.003	−.028	.017	−.073	−.002
3. Comm Freq – Mother → Pos Emotional Responses	−.034	.034	−.108	.027	−.025	.024	−.076	.020
4. Comm Freq – Mother → Neg Emotional Responses	.018	.033	−.047	.084	.016	.029	−.043	.072
5. Comm Freq – Father → Sexual Assertiveness	.002	.009	−.008	.030	.001	.007	−.007	.029
6. Comm Freq – Father → Safe-sex Competence	.005	.015	−.022	.042	.005	.016	−.0213	.045
7. Comm Freq – Father → Pos Emotional Responses	.008	.026	−.042	.064	.008	.026	−.039	.068
8. Comm Freq – Father → Neg Emotional Responses	−.022	.024	−.076	.022	−.025	.029	−.092	.025
9. Comm Freq – Friend → Sexual Assertiveness	.002	.010	−.011	.035	.001	.007	−.007	.024
10. Comm Freq – Friend → Safe-sex Competence	.000	.023	−.047	.046	.000	.016	−.034	.033
11. Comm Freq – Friend → Pos Emotional Responses	.015	.037	−.051	.099	.010	.027	−.037	.070
12. Comm Freq – Friend → Neg Emotional Responses	−.043	.039	−.126	.027	−.037	.033	−.107	.024

Notes: *$p < .05$. Comm = communication. Freq = frequency. Qual = quality. Pos = positive. Neg = Negative.

TABLE 4

Path estimates, standard errors and confidence intervals for models mediated by pleasure self-efficacy ($N = 209$)

	Unstandardised				Standardised			
Models	*a × b Effect*	*SE*	*Lower 95% CI*	*Upper 95% CI*	*a × b Effect*	*SE*	*Lower 95% CI*	*Upper 95% CI*
1. Comm Freq – Mother → Sexual Assertiveness	.030	.025	−.007	.094	.021	.017	−.005	.099
2. Comm Freq – Mother → Safe-sex Competence	.026	.026	−.016	.089	.019	.019	−.011	.065
3. Comm Freq – Mother → Pos Emotional Responses	.075*	.040	.002	.164	.055	.028	.002	.116
4. Comm Freq – Mother → Neg Emotional Responses	−.045*	.026	−.111	−.006	−.039	.022	−.096	−.006
5. Comm Freq – Father → Sexual Assertiveness	.042*	.023	.011	.104	.039	.019	.011	.089
6. Comm Freq – Father → Safe-sex Competence	.038*	.023	.006	.096	.038	.021	.007	.089
7. Comm Freq – Father → Pos Emotional Responses	.064*	.030	.016	.140	.063	.027	.017	.125
8. Comm Freq – Father → Neg Emotional Responses	−.042*	.022	−.000	−.010	−.049	.024	−.107	−.013
9. Comm Freq – Friend → Sexual Assertiveness	.056*	.028	.014	.126	.038	.018	.009	.084
10. Comm Freq – Friend → Safe-sex Competence	.048*	.027	.008	.115	.034	.019	.006	.082
11. Comm Freq – Friend → Pos Emotional Responses	.095*	.038	.028	.0177	.068	.027	.021	.126
12. Comm Freq – Friend → Neg Emotional Responses	−.061*	.027	−.131	−.022	−.052	.023	−.110	−.018

Notes: *$p < .05$. Comm = communication. Freq = frequency. Qual = quality. Pos = positive. Neg = Negative.

TABLE 5

Results of regressing safe-sex behavioural competence and sexual assertiveness on communication quality and sexual subjectivity ($N = 209$)

	Sexual assertiveness		*Safe-sex competence*		*Positive emotional responses*		*Negative emotional responses*	
Independent variables	B (*SE*)	β	B (*SE*)	β	B (*SE*)	β	B (*SE*)	β
Version	.00 (.10)	.00	−.16 (.11)	−.12	−.15 (.11)	−.10	.04 (.13)	.03
Gender	.34 (.12)	.28**	.07 (.12)	.05	.11 (.12)	.08	.27 (.15)	.17
Age	.04 (.04)	.06	.08 (.04)	.12	−.03 (.04)	−.05	.00 (.05)	.00
Relationship status	.27 (.09)	.21**	.14 (.09)	.10	.17 (.09)	.13	−.13 (.11)	−.08
Coital Experience	−.32 (.13)	−.18*	−.09 (.13)	−.04	.27 (.13)	.14*	−.15 (.16)	−.07
Comm quality – Mother	.03 (.08)	.03	.21 (.09)	.20*	−.12 (.08)	−.12	.04 (.10)	.03
Comm quality – Father	.04 (.09)	.05	.01 (.09)	.01	.19 (.09)	.19*	.06 (.11)	.05
Comm quality – Friend	.14 (.09)	.11	.27 (.09)	.20**	.15 (.09)	.11	−.17 (.11)	−.11
Sexual body esteem	.02 (.06)	.02	.14 (.07)	.14*	.19 (.06)	.20**	−.35 (.08)	−.30***
Pleasure self-efficacy	.19 (.07)	.18**	.12 (.07)	.11	.27 (.07)	.24**	−.17 (.09)	−.13

Notes: *$p < .05$. **$p < .01$. *** $p < .001$. Comm = Communication – Model 5: $F(10, 198) = 4.68$, $p < .001$, $R^2 = .19$; Model 6: $F(10, 198) = 5.07$, $p < .001$, $R^2 = .20$; Model 7: $F(10, 198) = 6.83$, $p < .001$, $R^2 = .26$; Model 8: $F(10, 198) = 5.42$, $p < .001$, $R^2 = .22$. Comm = Communication – Gender: 0 = males, 1 = females. Version: 0 = hard copy, 1 = online version. Relationship status: 0 = No partner, 1 = Current steady partner. Coital experience: 0 = No, 1 = Yes.

pleasure self-efficacy reported greater sexual assertiveness (see Table 5). For safe-sex behavioural competence, young adults with better communication quality with mother and friend, and greater sexual body esteem reported greater safe-sex competency. The variance accounted for in safe-sex competency was 20%.

Emotional responses to sexual experience. For positive emotional responses and communication quality, those with coital experience and those reporting better quality communication with their father reported more positive responses to their sexual experiences, as did participants with greater sexual body esteem and pleasure self-efficacy (see Table 5). For negative responses those with lower sexual body esteem reported more negative responses.

DISCUSSION

The purpose of the current study was to examine whether sex-related communication with mother, father and best friend was associated with sexual well-being, defined as safer sexual behaviour, more sexual assertiveness and more positive emotions (and fewer negative) in regard to their sexual behaviour. We also considered whether one's sexual self-perceptions, referred to as sexual subjectivity, would be associated with sexual well-being and might render some of these associations indirectly.

Communication frequency in high school, sexual well-being and sexual subjectivity

We found support for our hypothesis that more frequent communication in high school would be associated with greater sexual well-being. In our multivariate models, which considered age, relationship status, coital status and sexual subjectivity (sexual body-esteem, pleasure self-efficacy), young adults who retrospectively reported more frequent communication with their mothers and best friends in high school reported greater safe-sex competence. Those who reported more frequent communication with their fathers reported more positive emotional responses to sex. A possible explanation for these different associations between mother and father communication and their children's sexual well-being could be that the emphasis and content of sex-related communication differs when it involves mothers as compared to fathers. It is possible that communication from mothers underscores how to avoid risk more so than providing information about the pleasurable and desirable aspects of sex. In contrast, communication with fathers, although also likely to include some discussions about sexual risks, may be framed in a way that places more emphasis on the positive aspects of sexual behaviour. Previous qualitative research indicates that mothers provide more factual and safe-sex education compared to fathers (Nolin & Petersen, 1992), and that fathers express more positivity about sex than mothers (Hutchinson, 2002). No measure of past communication was associated with sexual assertiveness in the multivariate models. Although there has been no previous investigation of associations of communication with safe-sex behavioural competence and emotional responses to sex, these results are consistent with past research that parent-adolescent communication about sex is associated with decreased adolescent sexual risk behaviours (Aspy et al., 2007; Hutchinson, 2002). Furthermore, these findings suggest that communication with friends about sex during high school may also play a role in later safer-sex behaviour.

One explanation for why sex-related communication may be associated with sexual well-being comes from our analyses of sexual subjectivity in this study. We found that young adults higher in sexual subjectivity were higher in sexual well-being. In regression models, at least one element of sexual subjectivity was associated with each measure of sexual well-being. Furthermore, when indirect effects were tested, some small but significant indirect pathways were found between communication and sexual well-being via pleasure self-efficacy. There was also one significant indirect effect via sexual body esteem. Most notably, the indirect effects between communication frequency and both positive and negative emotional responses via pleasure self-efficacy were significant for mother, father and friend. These indirect relationships suggest that to some extent, more frequent communication with mother, father and best friend in adolescence helps formulate cognitions about personal sexual competency and pleasure, which then contributes to a young adult's ability to feel positive and behave assertively and safely in sexual experiences. However, these indirect pathways were small, and sexual subjectivity appears to account for only a small portion of the association between communication and sexual-well-being. This raises the question of whether there are other important factors to consider in future research. Previous research has found, for example, that cognitive autonomy, including autonomous decision-making capacity generally, and better quality romantic relationships (Zimmer-Gembeck, 2013) are also associated with greater sexual subjectivity. Thus communication about sex with parents and friends during high school might aid the development of autonomous functioning and result in more positive romantic relationships, which could also account for more positive sexual well-being in later life.

Quality of communication about sex

Our analyses of young adults' perceptions of the quality of their sex-related communication with parents and best friends revealed more numerous associations with sexual well-being. In multivariate analyses, youth who reported higher quality communication with their mothers and best friends reported more safe sex competence, and those who reported higher quality communication with their fathers had more positive emotional responses to sex.

These findings illustrate the importance of assessing communication with mothers separate from communication with fathers, and suggest that specific individuals play differing roles in informing young people's thoughts and behaviours around their sexual experience. Other research has shown that father communication with their adolescents may have different associations with sexual attitudes and behaviours than mother communication (Wright, Randall, & Arroyo, 2013).

Sexual subjectivity and sexual well-being

Although there were some differences across our models, in general the findings suggest that sexual subjectivity was more relevant as a correlate of greater sexual assertiveness and fewer negative emotional reactions to sex than was communication, whereas both communication and sexual subjectivity were relevant to safe-sex behavioural competence and positive emotional reactions to sex. Associations of greater sexual subjectivity with sexual assertiveness and fewer negative emotions suggest that behaving more assertively within the sexual domain may depend on positive feelings about personal desirability and entitlement, and this may help youth to avoid sex that is uncomfortable, unwanted, embarrassing or related to other negative emotions. Thus, esteem and feelings of efficacy and entitlement may allow youth to feel more confident in asserting their sexual needs and this reduces the negative emotions that can arise after sex, especially sexual behaviour that is risky or not wanted (Rosenthal et al., 1991). However, feeling more competent in safe-sex behaviour might benefit more from external information sources like family or friends who can provide specific, instructional information for sexual safety. In a similar way, it is possible that communication about emotions related to sex is specific, where parents and peers are positively biased in the emotional content they discuss in sexual conversations.

Gender, romantic status, coital experience and age

Young women and those in steady relationships felt more sexually assertive, but gender and romantic status were not associated with other measures of sexual well-being. Thus, the closeness of a steady relationship seems to provide an environment for greater sexual assertion. Regarding, gender, perhaps young women recognise sexual assertion as more necessary, as sexual interactions are often structured in such a way that they receive more sexual interest than young men, which requires them to be more discriminant in their choices and behaviours. However, past research has found Australian young men to be more assertive than women (Rosenthal et al., 1991) and many young women report that they do not feel assertive when it comes to choice about sexual behaviours and contraception (Rickert, Sanghvi, & Wiemann, 2002). Thus, this may be a historical difference, with young women now feeling more assertive than they did in the past. Further research is needed, however, to confirm such a conclusion.

Those with coital experience felt less sexually assertive, but, in one model, had more positive emotional responses to sex. The need for assertiveness may slightly decline after intercourse has been initiated, as young people may feel they have less choice or less need to be assertive once they have had this experience. Furthermore, it may be that those with intercourse experience feel more positive because of that very reason; their sexual encounters have included intercourse, which often brings a higher level of intimacy, while those without sexual intercourse experience have less positive, but not necessarily more negative, emotions to report in response to their sexual experience.

Finally, age was not associated with sexual well-being in any of the models. Although the age range of this study only spanned a few years, this does suggest that it is not age but rather sexual self-perceptions and social experiences that are most relevant to understanding sexual well-being in the late adolescent and very early adult years.

Limitations and conclusion

Although the findings do suggest that sex-related communication with others is associated with greater sexual well-being, there are some limitations of the current study. These limitations are the convenience sample, the use of a cross-sectional study design and the need to rely on some retrospective reports about frequency of communication in the past. These issues can reduce the generalisability of the study findings, and make it impossible to determine the direction of associations. For example, it is also plausible that quality communication about sex is promoted by greater sexual well-being, as much as the converse.

This study adds to a growing body of research on the development of sexual self-concept (O'Sullivan, Meyer-Bahlburg, & McKeague, 2006) and sexual subjectivity (Zimmer-Gembeck et al., 2011), by showing that young adults feel more capable of sexually safe behaviours and report more positive emotions related to sexual behaviour when they have more frequent communication about sex-related topics in high school, and currently perceive that their sexual communication with parents and best friends is of greater quality. Also, sexual subjectivity (sexual self esteem and self-perceptions of efficacy in achieving sexual pleasure) is uniquely associated with many aspects of sexual well-being. A fruitful direction for research will be to extend this study to examine the development of sexual well-being during and beyond adolescence. Identifying specific interactions with parents, friends and partners during adolescence, such as open communication about intimacy and related topics, will be important in such an approach. Such information has important basic theoretical implications, but could also be applied to improve sexual developmental pathways and well-being during adolescence and into later life.

REFERENCES

Akers, A. Y., Holland, C. L., & Bost, J. (2011). Interventions to improve parental communication about sex: a systematic review. *Pediatrics, 127*, 494–510. doi:10.1542/peds.2010-2194

Aspy, C. B., Vesely, S. K., Oman, R. F., Rodine, S., Marshall, L., & McLeroy, K. (2007). Parental communication and youth sexual behaviour. *Journal of Adolescence, 30*, 449–466. doi:10.1016/j.adolescence.2006.04.007

Bleakley, A., Hennessy, M., Fishbein, M., & Jordan, A. (2009). How sources of sexual information relate to adolescents' beliefs about sex. *American Journal of Health Behavior, 33*, 37–48. doi:10.5993/AJHB.33.1.4

Byers, E. S., & Rehman, U. S. (2014). Sexual well-being. In D. L. Tolman, L. M. Diamond, J. A. Bauermeister, W. H. George, J. G. Pfaus, & M. L. Ward (Eds.), *APA handbook of sexuality and psychology, Vol. 1: Person-based approaches* (pp. 317–337). Washington, DC. doi:10.1037/14193-011 American Psychological Association.

Connolly, J. A., Craig, W., Goldberg, A., & Pepler, D. (2004). Mixed-gender groups, dating, and romantic relationships in early adolescence. *Journal of Research in Adolescence, 14*, 185–207. doi:10.1111/j.1532-7795.2004.01402003.x

Feldman, S. S., & Rosenthal, D. A. (2000). The effect of communication characteristics on family members' perceptions of parents as sex educators. *Journal of Research on Adolescence, 10*, 119–150. doi:10.1207/SJRA1002_1

Fortenberry, J. D. (2014). Sexual learning, sexual experience, and healthy adolescent sex. In E. S. Lefkowitz & S. A. Vasilenko (Eds.), *Positive and negative outcomes of sexual behaviors. New Directions for Child and Adolescent Development* (Vol. 144, pp. 71–86). doi:10.1002/cad.20061/pdf

Guilamo-Ramos, V., Jaccard, J., Dittus, P., & Collins, S. (2008). Parent-adolescent communication about sexual intercourse: an analysis of maternal reluctance to communicate. *Health Psychology, 27*, 760–769. doi:10.1037/a0013833

Guzmán, B. L., Schlehofer-Sutton, M. M., Villanueva, C. M., Dello Stritto, M. E., Casad, B. J., & Feria, A. (2003). Let's talk about sex: How comfortable discussions about sex impact teen sexual behaviour. *Journal of Health Communication, 8*, 583–598. doi:10.1080/716100416

Halpern-Felsher, B. L., Kropp, R. Y., Boyer, C. B., Tschann, J. M., & Ellen, J. M. (2004). Adolescents' self-efficacy to communicate about sex: Its role in condom attitudes, commitment and use. *Adolescence, 39*, 443–456. Retrieved from http://search.proquest.com.libraryproxy griffith.edu griffith.edu.au/docview/195939590?accountid=14543

Harden, K. P. (2014). A sex-positive framework for research on adolescent sexuality. *Perspectives on Psychological Science, 9*, 455–469. doi:10.1177/1745691614535934

Horne, S., & Zimmer-Gembeck, M. J. (2006). The female sexual subjectivity inventory: Development and validation of a multidimensional inventory for late adolescents and emerging adults. *Psychology of Women Quarterly, 30*, 125–138. doi:10.1111/j.1471-6402.2006.00276.x

Hutchinson, M. K. (2002). The influence of sexual risk communication between parents and daughters on sexual risk behaviors. *Family Relations, 51*, 238–247. doi:10.1111/j.1741-3729.2002.00238.x

Hutchinson, M. K., & Cederbaum, J. A. (2011). Talking to daddy's little girl about sex: Daughters' reports of sexual communication and support from fathers. *Journal of Family Issues, 32*, 550–572. doi:10.1177/0192513X10384222

Lefkowitz, E. S., Boone, T. L., & Shearer, C. L. (2004). Communication with best friends about sex-related topics during emerging adulthood. *Journal of Youth and Adolescence, 33*, 339–351. doi:10.1023/B:JOYO.0000032642.27242.c1

Lefkowitz, E. S., & Espinosa-Hernandez, G. (2007). Sex-related communication with mothers and close friends during the transition to university. *Journal of Sex Research, 44*, 17–27. doi:10.1080/00224490709336789

Mauras, C. P., Grolnick, W. S., & Friendly, R. W. (2013). Time for 'the Talk'... Now what? Autonomy support and structure in mother–daughter conversations about sex. *The Journal of Early Adolescence, 33*, 458–481. doi:10.1177/0272431612449385

Nolin, M. J., & Petersen, K. K. (1992). Gender Differences in Parent–Child Communication about Sexuality An Exploratory Study. *Journal of Adolescent Research, 7*, 59–79. doi:10.1177/074355489271005

O'Sullivan, L. F., Meyer-Bahlburg, H. F. L., & McKeague, I. W. (2006). The development of the sexual self-concept inventory for early adolescent girls. *Psychology of Women Quarterly, 30*, 139–149. doi:10.1111/j.1471-6402.2006.00277.x

Pearson, J. (2006). Personal control, self-efficacy in sexual negotiation and contraceptive risk among adolescents: The role of gender. *Sex Roles, 54*, 615–625. doi:10.1007/s11199-006-9028-9

Rickert, V. I., Sanghvi, R., & Wiemann, C. M. (2002). Is lack of sexual assertiveness among adolescent and young adult women a cause for concern? *Perspectives on Sexual and Reproductive Health, 34*, 178–183. http://74.8.60.202/pubs/journals/3417802.pdf10.2307/3097727

Rosenthal, D. A., & Feldman, S. S. (1999). The importance of importance: Parent–adolescent communication about sexuality. *Journal of Adolescence, 22*, 835–851. doi:10.1006/jado.1999.0279

Rosenthal, D., Moore, S., & Flynn, I. (1991). Adolescent self-efficacy, self-esteem and sexual risk-taking. *Journal of Community & Applied Social Psychology, 1*, 77–88. doi:10.1002/casp.2450010203

Schwartz, I. M. (1998). First coital affective reaction scale. In C. Davis, W. L. Yarber, R. Bauserman, G. E. Schreer, & S. L. Davis (Eds.), *Handbook of sexuality related measures* (pp. 127–128). Thousand Oaks: Sage Publications.

Sneed, C. D., Somoza, C. G., Jones, T., & Alfaro, S. (2013). Topics discussed with mothers and fathers for parent-child sex communication among African-American adolescents. *Sex Education, 13*, 450–458. doi:10.1080/14681811.2012.757548

Sprecher, S., Harris, G., & Meyers, A. (2008). Perceptions of sources of sex education and targets of sex communication: sociodemographic and cohort effects. *Journal of Sex Research, 45*, 17–26. doi:10.1080/00224490701629522

Tolman, D. L. (2002). *Dilemmas of desire*. Boston, MA: Harvard University Press.

Tolman, D. L., & McClelland, S. I. (2011). Normative sexuality development in adolescence: A decade in review, 2000-2009. *Journal of Research on Adolescence, 21*, 242–255. doi:10.1111/j.1532-7795.2010.00726.x

Warren, C. (1995). Parent-child communication about sex. In T. J. Socha G & H. Stamp (Eds.), *Parents, children and communication: Frontiers of theory and research* (pp. 173–201). Mahwah, NJ: Erlbaum.

Wright, P. J., Randall, A. K., & Arroyo, A. (2013). Father-daughter communication about sex moderates the association between exposure to MTV's 16 and pregnant/teen mom and female students' pregnancy-risk behavior. *Sexuality & Culture, 17*, 50–66. doi: 10.1007/s12119-012-9137-2

Zimmer-Gembeck, M. J. (2013). Young females' sexual self-efficacy: Associations with personal autonomy and the couple relationship. *Sexual Health, 10*, 204–210. http://dx.doi.org/10.1071/SH12139

Zimmer-Gembeck, M. J., Ducat, W. H., & Boislard-Pepin, M. (2011). A prospective study of young females' sexual subjectivity: associations with age, sexual behavior, and dating. *Archives of Sexual Behaviour, 40*, 927–938. doi:10.1007/s10508-011-9751-3

Zimmer-Gembeck, M. J, Ducat, W., & Collins, W. A. (2011). Autonomy development during adolescence. In B. B. Brown & M. Prinstein (Eds.), *Encyclopedia of Adolescence* (pp. 66–76). New York: Academic Press.

Zimmer-Gembeck, M. J., & French, J. (in press). Associations of sexual subjectivity with global and sexual well-being: A new measure for young men. *Archives of Sexual Behavior* (pp. 113–122). doi:10.1007/s10508-014-0387-y

Zimmer-Gembeck, M. J., See, L., & O'Sullivan, L. F. (2015). Young women's satisfaction with sex and romance, and emotional reactions to sex: associations with sexual entitlement, efficacy, and situational factors. *Emerging Adulthood, 3*, 113–122. doi:10.1177/2167696814548060

Parent and peer predictors of adolescents' sexual development: Can parents buffer peer influence?

Wim Beyers, Evlin Veryser, and Elke Verlee

Ghent University, Belgium

While lot of parents aim to delay sexual development of their children, peers often stimulate sexual development. How do adolescents deal with these differing social influences? Literature suggests that positive parenting is a buffer against peer influence. In this study, 992 Belgian adolescents (50% girls; 12 to 20 years) reported on own experience and timing of sexual behaviour, perceived parenting and descriptive and injunctive peer norms. Regressions revealed that parental behavioural control predicted later timing of sexual debut. Only descriptive peer norms predicted more sexual experience. The parents-as-buffer hypothesis was not supported. Four parenting by peer interactions, however, showed that positive parenting intensifies peer prediction of sexual development, particularly during late adolescence. Together, this study emphasizes the importance of parenting strategies that enable adolescents to make their own autonomous decisions (regarding sexual and other behaviours) within the context of peer relations, where various types of influence may play a role.

Sexual development is a normative developmental task in adolescence (De Graaf, Beyers, & van Acker, 2012). An important part of it is the development of a wide range of sexual behaviours. By age 20, the large majority of adolescents have experience with a broad set of sexual behaviours, ranging from intimate kissing, masturbation, touching and fondling to sexual intercourse. Nevertheless, substantial interindividual differences exist in the timing of sexual debut. Which factors explain these differences was the focus of lot of research in past decades, with particular attention to individual and societal factors (Small &

No potential conflict of interest was reported by the authors.

Luster, 1994). However, the meso-context of adolescents developing their sexuality, that is, interactions between different actors in the micro-context, such as parents and peers, received less attention (Sennott & Mollborn, 2011).

Parents or peers as socializers of sexual development in adolescence

Studies about parental influence on teen sexual behaviour showed a mixed pattern. Most parents aim to delay first sexual experience in their adolescent children (White & Warner, 2015). Nevertheless, most teens have experience with sexual behaviour during adolescence (e.g., in Belgium, the country with relatively liberal sexual attitudes (Nicolosi et al., 2004) where this study was performed, at 17.7 years, 50% of the adolescents report experience with sexual intercourse (coitus); at age 21 this is 89%; De Graaf et al., 2012). However, research shows that parents can delay onset of sexual experience (Buhi & Goodson, 2007). A recent review on parenting and adolescents' sexual development (De Graaf, Vanwesenbeeck, Woertman, & Meeus, 2011) showed that higher levels of parental support (i.e., warmth, responsiveness), behavioural control (i.e., discipline, setting rules and expectations, and providing predictable consequences for adolescents' transgressions) and knowledge predict a delay of first sexual intercourse. However, the same review also showed that when parents are psychologically controlling (i.e., using intrusive and manipulative control; Barber, 1996), adolescents show earlier debut of sex.

Research about peer influences on sexual development is more straightforward. Teens' sexual behaviour is strongly embedded in peer context (Fasula & Miller, 2006) and perceived sexual experience (descriptive norms) and attitudes of peers (injunctive norms) are both possible sources of peer influence on adolescent's sexual development (Buhi & Goodson, 2007). Kinsman, Romer, Furstenberg, and Schwarz (1998) showed that the strongest predictor of a high intention to initiate sexual behaviour was the belief that most friends already had sexual intercourse. A recent meta-analysis (Van de Bongardt, Reitz, Sandfort, & Deković, 2014) also showed that descriptive norms were more strongly related to adolescent sexual activity than injunctive norms.

Parent and peer context do not stand apart

Very often, parents and peers are two competing socializing sources for the sexually developing adolescent (Sennott & Mollborn, 2011). Up to this date, only four studies examined combined influence of parents and peers on adolescent sexual development, and converged in the conclusion that parents can buffer influence of peer norms on sexual intention or initiation. Focusing on everyday general parenting, as done in the present study, East, Khoo, and Reyes (2006) showed that parental involvement and behavioural control during early adolescence buffered against teenage pregnancy for Latina an African-American girls under conditions of strong peer risk. Three other studies confirmed that lack of communication with parents about sex makes adolescents turn to peers, whereas frequent or high-quality communication with parents buffered peer influence (Fasula & Miller, 2006; Van de Bongardt, de Graaf, Reitz, & Deković, 2014; Whitaker & Miller, 2000).

The role of adolescents' age and gender

Earlier studies started from a risk perspective on adolescent sexuality and focused on early adolescence and the intention or initiation of sexual intercourse. In this study, we used a sample of Belgian adolescents, comprising early, middle and late adolescents, all of which have sexual experience. This allowed us to study parent and peer predictors and their interactions on sexual behaviour across the complete age range of adolescence. Having a sample perfectly balanced on gender also allowed for testing interactions with gender.

As many studies show, sexual behaviour develops progressively during adolescence (e.g., De Graaf et al., 2012). At the same time, with increasing age parents become less controlling and more autonomy-supportive (for reviews, see Collins, 1990; Steinberg, 2001), whereas parental responsiveness and support gradually decrease (Meeus, Iedema, Maassen, & Engels, 2005). From this we can derive that parental influence on sexual development might be strongest in early adolescence.

Less straightforward changes occur in the socializing influence of peers. On the one hand, the strength of sexual peer norms peaks during early and middle adolescence (Fraser, 1997). On the other hand, adolescents' resistance to peer pressure starts increasing from middle adolescence onwards (Steinberg & Monahan, 2007). Together, this means that particularly in early and middle adolescence influence of peers on sexual behaviour might be salient (Treboux & Busch-Rossnagel, 1995). Alternatively, the relationship between sexual peer norms and adolescents' sexual behaviour might be stronger at ages where sexual activity becomes more normative, that is, middle and late adolescence (Van de Bongardt, Reitz, et al., 2014).

Finally, with respect to parent by peer interactions, theorizing and research on the possible moderating role of age is non-existing. However, in Social Domain Theory, Smetana (1995) stated that adolescents increasingly consider their friendships and peer relations as part of their personal domain. The same applies to sexual behaviour (Shaw, Wainryb, & Smetana, 2014). So, with increasing age, adolescents view their parents' interventions in the domains of peer relations or sexuality illegitimate and stress their independent decision making in these domains more. Consequently, parents might be more successful in buffering peer influence on sexual behavior during early adolescence, but sure not during late adolescence.

Previous research reported that female adolescents experience more parental vigilance regarding friendships, sure when these are intimate relationships involving sexuality (Faulkner & Schaller, 2007). Girls also are more resistant to peer influence than boys (Steinberg & Monahan, 2007). However, unlike studies investigating age differences, gender received much less attention, with several studies examining parent and peer influences on sexual development only in female adolescents (e.g., Treboux & Busch-Rossnagel, 1995).

Hypotheses

Regarding parent main effects, based on the above cited literature we expect parental responsiveness, behavioural control and autonomy support to be associated with less and later onset of sexual experience, whereas parental psychological control might predict earlier onset (De Graaf et al., 2011). Regarding peer influence, we expect stronger effects of descriptive peer norms, predicting more sexual experience and earlier timing (Van de Bongardt, Reitz, et al., 2014). Parent influence is expected to be most salient in early and middle adolescence, compared to late adolescence (Steinberg, 2001). Influence of sexual peer norms on one hand can be stronger in early adolescence, when resistance to peer pressure is low (Steinberg & Monahan, 2007). Alternatively, sexual peer influence might be stronger in middle and late adolescence, compared to early adolescence (Van de Bongardt, Reitz, et al., 2014), because sexual behaviour is more normative at later ages. Parent influence on sexual behaviour is expected to be stronger in female adolescents (Faulkner & Schaller, 2007), whereas peer influence is expected to be stronger in male adolescents (Steinberg & Monahan, 2007).

Finally, we expect complex associations between adolescents' awareness of these two socializing sources on their sexual development. In line with the few existing studies, we hypothesize that parents by being warm, supportive and behaviourally controlling, can buffer peer influence on sexual development (the parents-as-buffer hypothesis). If buffering occurs, this might be stronger in early and middle adolescence and females, compared to late adolescence and males.

METHODS

Participants

From an initial sample of 1217 adolescents, 992 adolescents that reported at least some sexual experience were selected for this study. They were aged 12–20 years (*M* = 15 years and 7 months; *SD* = 22 months), with an equal number of boys and girls. Three age groups were distinguished: early adolescence (12 years to 14 years 6 months; *n* = 324), middle adolescence (14 years 7 months to 17 year 6 months; *n* = 476) and late adolescence (17 year 7 months to 20 years; *n* = 192).

Of all adolescents, 67% were students in the academic track, 15% in technical education, and 18% were in vocational training. Of these adolescents, 73% grew up in intact families (i.e., with both parents present). Most of them (76%) reported having (had) a romantic relationship.

Part of the data was missing (2.9%). However, Little's (1988) MCAR-test (normed χ^2 of 2.11) suggested that missing most likely occurred at random. Therefore, missing data were estimated using the EM-algorithm (Schafer, 1997). Given the large sample size and number of statistical tests, effects in the total sample were considered significant when $p < .01$.

Measures

All self-report measures were either developed for the purpose of this study or independently translated from English in Dutch by three researchers, reaching a final translation through discussion.

Sexual behaviour. Based on earlier work (De Graaf et al., 2012; Rosenthal & Smith, 1997) and a qualitative pilot study with 30 adolescents (asking what they consider to be sex), participants were asked to report their experience (0 = *no experience*; 1 = *experience*) with 13 sexual behaviours that were formulated in youth language, that is, (1) kissing on mouth, (2) sexual excitement, (3) masturbation, (4) French kissing, (5) touching above cloths, (6) touching under cloths, (7) touching each other's genitals, (8) jacking someone off, (9) fingering, (10) vaginal intercourse, (11) fellatio, (12) cunnilingus, and (13) anal intercourse. When experience was reported, the onset age for each of these behaviours was assessed.

Based on this measure, three variables were calculated. Non-genital experience (mean of items 1–6 above; Cronbach's $\alpha = .86$; $M = 0.74$; $SD = 0.30$) and genital experience (items 7–13; $\alpha = .94$; $M = 0.29$; $SD = 0.37$) were differentiated based on a principal component analysis. Two factors had eigenvalues >1 and together explained 68% of the variance in the experience data, with factor loadings after oblimin rotation ranging between .54 and .77 for non-genital experience and .53 and .89. for genital experience. Non-genital and genital sexual experience were correlated, as expected ($r = .45$; $p < .001$), although the size of the correlation underscores the differentiation of the two factors. Higher scores indicate experience with more types of sexual behaviour.

Timing of sexual debut was based on Flemish norm data by age and gender ($N = 3487$ adolescents; De Graaf et al., 2012). Raw scores of age at first experience for all reported sexual behaviours were recoded to *early* (1 *SD* below average age in norm data; coded as 0), *modal* (between 1 *SD* below and above average; (1) or *late* (1 *SD* above average, or not yet experience at that late age; (2) and then averaged across available timing scores. Cronbach's alpha of the timing measure was .95 and no evidence was found for more than one factor, with a single factor explaining 64% of the variance in the timing data. In this sample 17% of the adolescents were relatively early ($M < 0.50$) in the timing of their sexual debut, 71% were modal ($0.51 > M < 1.50$), and 7% were late ($M > 1.51$).

Perceived parenting. Perceived parenting was measured with items from the Louvain Adolescent Perceived Parenting Scale (LAPPS; Soenens et al., 2004), assessing four parenting style dimensions using a 5-point Likert scale, ranging from 1 (*completely untrue*) to 5 (*completely true*). Responsiveness measures the amount of warmth and support provided by parents (7 items, e.g., "My parents make me feel better after talking over my worries with them"; Cronbach's $\alpha = .89$; $M = 3.74$; $SD = 0.81$). Behavioural control refers to providing discipline by parents (7 items, e.g., "My parents believe in having a lot of rules and sticking with them"; $\alpha = .78$; $M = 3.35$; $SD = 0.69$). Parental psychological control taps parents' use of intrusive and manipulative control (7 items, e.g., "My parents avoid looking at me when I have disappointed them"; $\alpha = .77$; $M = 2.42$; $SD = 0.72$). Finally, autonomy support measures support of volitional functioning (5 items, e.g., "My parents help me to choose my own direction"; $\alpha = .69$; $M = 3.64$; $SD = 0.65$). Previous research supported the reliability and construct validity of the LAPPS (e.g., Soenens et al., 2004).

Descriptive and injunctive peer norms. Adolescents reported on their perception of peers' and friends' experience during the past month with the sexual behaviours above, using a 5-point Likert scale ranging from 1 (*absolutely not*) to 5 (*yes, indeed*). Cronbach's alpha for descriptive non-genital norms was .89 ($M = 3.84$; $SD = 1.01$), and .88 for descriptive genital norms ($M = 1.95$; $SD = 1.72$). Similarly, adolescents were asked to indicate whether or not their peers think these sexual behaviours are OK for adolescents at their age, using the same Likert scale. Injunctive peer norms towards non-genital ($M = 4.16$; $SD = 0.87$) and genital sexual experience ($M = 2.79$; $SD = 1.29$) were reliable ($\alpha = .89$ and .84, respectively).

Social desirability. To control for adolescents' social desirable answering, 16 items based on the original measure by Crowne and Marlowe (1960) were used ($\alpha = .67$; $M = 0.42$; $SD = 0.18$). Using a forced choice answering format (0 = *wrong*; 1 = *correct*) adolescents answered items such as "I sometimes get annoyed when being asked a favour".

Procedure

Participating adolescents were recruited through secondary schools in the Dutch-speaking part of Belgium. Data were gathered in small class groups and took no longer than 50 min. Active adolescent consent and passive informed parental consent was obtained. Anonymity was guaranteed, and privacy was assured by providing enough empty space between participants.

RESULTS

Parent and peer main predictions

Table 1 shows results of a hierarchical regression analysis, predicting non-genital and genital sexual experience and timing of sexual debut. Background variables (age, gender, educational level and social desirability) were entered in Step 1 and explained substantial part of the variance in the dependent variables. Older adolescents showed more sexual experience. Gender was unrelated to sexual experience or timing. Adolescents in higher educational levels showed less genital experience and later timing of sexual debut. Finally, social desirability was negatively related to both non-genital and genital sexual experience, and was associated with later timing of sexual debut.

In Step 2 all parent and peer predictors were added in the models. As shown in Table 1, after controlling for the background variables these predictors explained a small but significant part of the variance in sexual experience and timing. Perceived behavioural control by parents predicted a later timing of sexual debut.

TABLE 1
Hierarchical regression results of parent and peer main effects on sexual experience and timing

	Non-genital experience		*Genital experience*		*Timing of sexual debut*[a]	
	ΔR^2	β	ΔR^2	β	ΔR^2	β
Step 1	.34***		.40***		.17***	
Age		.50***		.58***		.43***
Gender		.04		−.01		−.06
Educational level		−.04		−.07**		.12***
Social Desirability		−.22***		−.12***		.08**
Step 2	.07***		.05***		.02**	
Parental responsiveness		−.04		−.04		.06
Parental behavioural control		−.01		−.03		.10**
Parental psychological control		.04		.01		−.03
Parental autonomy support		−.03		−.00		−.04
Peer non-genital experience		.16***		−.01		−.00
Peer genital experience		.05		.30***		−.01
Peer non-genital attitudes		.10		−.06		−.11
Peer genital attitudes		.09		.08		−.05

$^{**}p < .01$, $^{***}p < .001$.

[a] High scores indicate later timing of sexual debut.

Adolescents experiencing strong descriptive norms reported more non-genital as well as genital experience.

Additional interaction analyses with gender and age (48 interactions tested) revealed only one significant interaction with age ($\beta = .15$; $p < .01$), that is, descriptive genital norms predicted own genital experience, but more strongly in early adolescence, compared to middle and late adolescence (β's $= .42$, $p < .001$; $.32, p < .001$; and $.21, p < .01$, respectively). None of the interactions with gender were significant.

Parent by peer interactions

A total of 48 interactions between parenting and peer norms were tested, using the hierarchical regression approach suggested by Aiken and West (1991). Background variables were entered in Step 1, centered main effects in Step 2, and product terms assessing interactions in Step 3, one by one, given the large number of interactions. For significant interactions unstandardized gradients of simple slopes (*b*) were calculated at meaningful values of the moderator, that is, $M - 1$SD and $M + 1$SD. Additionally, significant interactions were plotted using the two-way standardized worksheet by Dawson (2014) and appear in Figure 1.

Four interactions were significant (Table 2), all predicting timing of sexual debut. Strong descriptive and injunctive non-genital norms predicted earlier

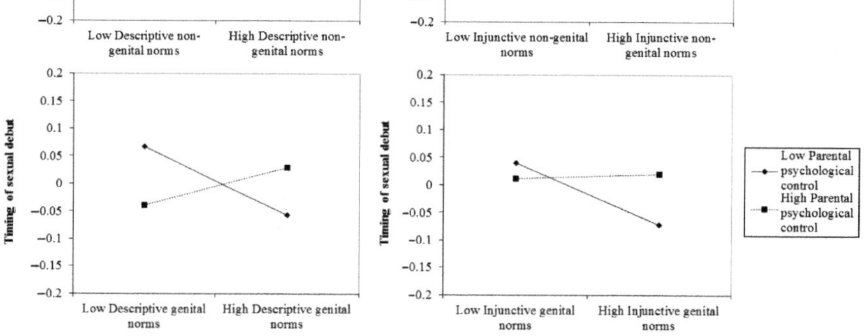

Figure 1. Standardized simple slope analyses (Dawson, 2014) of significant interaction effects between parenting and peer factors on the timing of adolescents' sexual debut. High scores on the dependent variable indicate later timing.

TABLE 2

Hierarchical regression results of parent by peer interactions on sexual development

	Non-genital experience		*Genital experience*		*Timing of sexual debut*	
	t	*β*	*t*	*β*	*t*	*β*
Responsiveness × Peer non-genital experience	2.37	.06	−0.55	−.01	−2.52	−.07
Responsiveness × Peer genital experience	1.02	.03	−2.28	−.06	−1.96	−.06
Responsiveness × Peer non-genital attitudes	2.58	.07	0.87	.02	−2.35	−.07
Responsiveness × Peer genital attitudes	1.28	.04	−1.60	−.04	−2.27	.07
Behavioural control × Peer non-genital experience	0.13	.00	−0.45	−.01	1.55	.05
Behavioural control × Peer genital experience	1.54	.04	−0.10	−.03	1.18	.04
Behavioural control × Peer non-genital attitudes	0.82	.02	0.68	.02	1.22	.04
Behavioural control × Peer genital attitudes	1.36	.04	−0.17	−.00	1.94	.06
Psychological Control × Peer non-genital experience	−2.12	−.05	0.29	.01	2.19	.07
Psychological Control × Peer genital experience	−1.80	−.05	0.19	.00	3.41	.10***
Psychological Control × Peer non-genital attitudes	−0.19	−.01	0.64	.02	1.41	.04
Psychological Control × Peer genital attitudes	−1.05	−.03	0.66	.02	2.63	.08**
Autonomy support × Peer non-genital experience	2.38	.06	0.33	.01	−2.96	−.09**
Autonomy support × Peer genital experience	0.24	.01	−0.07	−.00	−1.75	−.05
Autonomy support × Peer non-genital attitudes	0.73	.02	0.10	.00	−2.66	−.08**
Autonomy support × Peer genital attitudes	−0.97	−.03	−0.42	−.01	−2.30	−.07

$^{**}p < .01$, $^{***}p < .001$.

timing of sexual debut, but only when parental autonomy support (AS) was high (Figure 1, top; descriptive peer norms: low AS: $b = .01$, $p = .74$; high AS: $b = -.08, p < .01$; injunctive peer norms: low AS: $b = -.02, p = .40$; high AS: $b = -.11, p < .001$). Similarly, strong descriptive and injunctive genital norms predicted earlier timing of sexual debut, but only when parental psychological control (PC) was low (Figure 1, bottom; descriptive peer norms: low PC: $b = -.06$, $p < .01$; high PC: $b = .03$, $p = .24$; injunctive peer norms: low PC: $b = -.06$, $p < .01$; high PC: $b = .00$, $p = .85$).

Additional three-way interactions with gender or age (96 interactions) resulted in three interactions with age being significant, all predicting genital sexual experience. First, age moderated the parental responsiveness by descriptive non-genital norms interaction ($\beta = .09$; $p < .01$), indicating that only in late adolescence ($n = 192$; $\beta = .14$; $p < .05$) this parent by peer interaction emerged, with descriptive non-genital norms associated with more genital sexual experience when parental responsiveness was high ($b = .20$; $p < .01$) but with slightly less genital sexual experience when parental responsiveness was low ($b = -.05$; $p < .05$). In early ($n = 324$; $\beta = -.01$; $p = .89$) and middle adolescence ($n = 476$; $\beta = -.00$; $p = .99$) this interaction was not significant. Second, age moderated the parental responsiveness by injunctive non-genital norms interaction ($\beta = .08$; $p < .01$), indicating that only in late ($\beta = .08$; $p < .05$) and middle adolescence ($\beta = .10$; $p < .01$) this parent by peer interaction was significant, with injunctive non-genital norms predicting more genital sexual experience when parental responsiveness was high ($b = .09$; $p < .05$, and .47; $p < .01$ in middle and late adolescence, respectively) but not when parental responsiveness was low ($b = .02$; $p = .41$, and $-.07$; $p < .01$). In early adolescence this parent by peer interaction was not significant ($\beta = -.05$; $p = .49$). Finally, age moderated the parental psychological control by descriptive genital norms interaction ($\beta = .11$; $p < .01$), indicating that only in late adolescence ($\beta = -.25$; $p < .01$) this parent by peer interaction emerged, with descriptive genital norms predicting more genital experience when parental psychological control was low ($b = .35$; $p < .01$) but less when parental psychological control was high ($b = .11$; $p < .05$). In early ($\beta = .07$; $p = .33$) and middle adolescence ($\beta = -.04$; $p = .58$) this interaction was not significant. No significant three-way interactions with gender emerged.

DISCUSSION

In this study we examined parent and peer predictors of sexual experience and timing of adolescents having at least some sexual experience. Both main effects and parent by peer interactions were investigated. In contrast to previous studies (e.g., Buhi & Goodson, 2007), after controlling for relevant background variables such as adolescents' age, educational level and social desirable answering, little evidence was found for parental predictors of sexual experience or timing.

Only one small association was found, that is, when parents have a clear set of rules and expectations (behavioural control), onset of sexual experience was delayed to some extent. Contrary to what we expected, adolescents' age or gender did not moderate these results, showing that parental prediction of adolescents' sexual development was similar for boys and girls throughout adolescence.

In line with earlier research (e.g., Kinsman et al., 1998; Van de Bongardt, Reitz, & Deković, 2012) more evidence was found for peer prediction of sexual behaviour and timing. Particularly adolescents' sexual experience was predicted by descriptive peer norms, confirming that teens' sexual behaviour is embedded in peer networks (Fasula & Miller, 2006). Results also showed that prediction by descriptive norms decreases with age, confirming that resistance to peer influence on genital experience increases linearly between ages 12 and 20 (Steinberg & Monahan, 2007). No moderation by gender was found, so peer influence is similar for boys and girls.

However, as mentioned before, parent and peer contexts do not stand apart. Contrary to expectations and previous studies (East et al., 2006), none of the four interactions found in the total sample supported the parents-as-buffer hypothesis. Rather, all interactions converged in the conclusion that positive parenting, that is, parents supporting adolescents' autonomy and refraining from using intrusive control, intensifies peer influence. Interactions with age confirmed this conclusion, and showed that this pattern of interactions (positive parenting intensifying the influence of peer norms) primarily occurred in late adolescence, a period in which sexual behaviour is normative (De Graaf et al., 2012). These interactions underscore the idea that sexual behaviour (Shaw et al., 2014) as well as peers and friends (Smetana, 1995) are part of adolescents' personal domain, which parents are supposed to respect (Smetana, 2006). Already Rosenthal and Smith (1997) showed in a sample of 15- and 16-year olds a strong connection between sexual timetables and timetables of autonomy, with autonomy defined in that study as independence from parents. As put forward by De Graaf et al. (2011), adolescents who grow up in autonomy-supportive families, are more aware of their own needs, and more able to express them in relationships with peers, with whom they share their sexual experiences. And, as our results confirmed, this is true for both boys and girls.

Of course, despite having a large sample, a broad age range and measuring multiple sexual behaviours in this study, also some limitations are evident. This study was performed in Belgium, a country with relatively liberal sexual attitudes, though not all parents have a positive view on teen sexuality. Nevertheless, particularly in this type of context, adolescents might consider their sexual behaviour as part of their personal domain. In other countries, where adolescent sexuality is more considered a risk and strong societal pressure limits adolescents' autonomous sexual development (e.g., Latin and African-American girls; East et al., 2006), their sexuality might comprise a lot of moral concerns

(Shaw et al., 2014). Further, the literature (e.g., Doty, Willoughby, Lindahl, & Malik, 2010) suggests that some of the socializing processes investigated in this study might differ between heterosexual and non-heterosexual identified youths, for instance non-heterosexual youths might primarily be influenced by support from same-sex attracted peers, less so by support from parents or other peers. Unfortunately, sexual orientation was not assessed in this study. Next, overall adolescent self-report in these studies, also about parenting styles, might have inflated some of the findings and results in social desirable answering, which in the case of sexuality is reporting less sexual experience and later timing, even in a relatively liberal country as Belgium. Finally, the cross-sectional design of this study limits developmental conclusions and raises questions about direction of effects. For instance, although we conclude that parental behavioural control delays sexual timing, the truth might be the other way around, with parents being observers, that react to what happens with their adolescent children.

Nevertheless, an important conclusion remains. In order to understand socializing influences of parents and peers, we need to examine how they interact to create combined effects on adolescent sexual behaviour (Crosby & Miller, 2002). When we do this, a complex picture emerges that puts a challenge for parents guiding their adolescent children in their sexual development. On one hand, parents want and have to protect their children from the possible dangers involved in this part of development, including premature and unsafe sex. They can do this by providing clear rules and expectations (i.e., behavioural control). On the other hand, the findings of this study emphasize the importance of parenting strategies that enable adolescents to make their own autonomous decisions (regarding sexual and other behaviours) within the context of their peer relations, where various types of influence may play a role. As the peer management literature shows (Mounts, 2002; Soenens, Vansteenkiste, Smits, Lowet, & Goossens, 2007; Tilton-Weaver & Galambos, 2003), parents can do this by guiding and supporting, that is, talk with children about their expectations, norms and values concerning friendships, and encouraging specific friendships and providing space where their adolescents can interact with friends.

REFERENCES

Aiken, L. S., & West, S. G. (1991). *Multiple regression: Testing and interpreting interactions.* Thousand Oaks, CA: Sage.

Barber, B. K. (1996). Parental psychological control: Revisiting a neglected construct. *Child Development, 67,* 3296–3319. doi:10.2307/1131780

Buhi, E. R., & Goodson, P. (2007). Predictors of adolescent sexual behavior and intention: A theory-guided systematic review. *Journal of Adolescent Health, 40*, 4–21. doi:10.1016/j.jadohealth.2006.09.027

Collins, W. A. (1990). Parent–child relationships in the transition to adolescence: Continuity and change interaction, affect, and cognition. In R. Montemayor, G. R. Adams, & T. P. Gullotta (Eds.), *From childhood to adolescence: A transitional period?* (pp. 85–106). Newbury Park, CA: Sage.

Crosby, R. A., & Miller, K. S. (2002). Family influences on adolescent females' sexual health. In G. M. Wingood & R. J. DiClemente (Eds.), *Handbook of women's sexual and reproductive health* (pp. 113–127). New York: Plenum.

Crowne, D. P., & Marlowe, D. (1960). A new scale of social desirability independent of psychopathology. *Journal of Consulting Psychology, 24*, 349–354. doi:10.1037/h0047358

Dawson, J. F. (2014). Moderation in management research: What, why, when, and how. *Journal of Business and Psychology, 29*, 1–19. doi:10.1007/s10869-013-9308-7

De Graaf, H., Beyers, W., & van Acker, J. (2012). De seksuele carrière van Nederlandse en Vlaamse jongeren. *Kind & Adolescent, 33*, 179–187. doi:10.1007/s12453-012-0024-2

De Graaf, H., Vanwesenbeeck, I., Woertman, L., & Meeus, W. (2011). Parenting and adolescents' sexual development in Western societies. *European Psychologist, 16*, 21–31. doi:10.1027/1016-9040/a000031

Doty, N. D., Willoughby, B. L. B., Lindahl, K. M., & Malik, N. M. (2010). Sexuality related social support among lesbian, gay, and bisexual youth. *Journal of Youth and Adolescence, 39*, 1134–1147. doi:10.1007/s10964-010-9566-x

East, P. L., Khoo, S. T., & Reyes, B. T. (2006). Risk and protective factors predictive of adolescent pregnancy: A longitudinal, prospective study. *Applied Developmental Science, 10*, 188–199. doi:10.1207/s1532480xads1004_3

Fasula, A. M., & Miller, K. S. (2006). African-American and Hispanic adolescents' intentions to delay first intercourse: Parental communication as a buffer for sexually active peers. *Journal of Adolescent Health, 38*, 193–200. doi:10.1016/j.jadohealth.2004.12.009

Faulkner, J., & Schaller, M. (2007). Nepotistic nosiness: Inclusive fitness and vigilance of kin members' romantic relationships. *Evolution and Human Behavior, 28*, 430–438. doi:10.1016/j.evolhumbehav.2007.06.001

Fraser, M. (1997). *Risk and resilience in childhood: An ecological perspective*. Washington, DC: NASW.

Kinsman, S. B., Romer, D., Furstenberg, F. F., & Schwarz, D. F. (1998). Early sexual initiation: The role of peer norms. *Pediatrics, 102*, 1185–1192. doi:10.1542/peds.102.5.1185

Little, R. (1988). A test of missing completely at random for multivariate data with missing values. *Journal of the American Statistical Association, 83*, 1198–1202. doi:10.1080/01621459.1988.10478722

Meeus, W., Iedema, J., Maassen, G., & Engels, R. (2005). Separation-individuation revisited: On the interplay of parent–adolescent relations, identity and emotional adjustment in adolescence. *Journal of Adolescence, 28*, 89–106. doi:10.1016/j.adolescence.2004.07.003

Mounts, N. S. (2002). Parental management of adolescent peer relationships in context: The role of parenting style. *Journal of Family Psychology, 16*, 58–69. doi:10.1037/0893-3200.16.1.58

Nicolosi, A., Laumann, E. O., Glasser, D. B., Moreira, E. D., Paik, A., & Gingell, C. (2004). Sexual behavior and sexual dysfunctions after age 40: The Global Study of Sexual Attitudes and Behaviors. *Adult Urology, 64*, 991–997. doi:10.1016/j.urology.2004.06.055

Rosenthal, D. A., & Smith, A. M. A. (1997). Adolescent sexual timetables. *Journal of Youth and Adolescence, 26*, 619–636. doi:10.1023/A:1024538123804

Schafer, J. L. (1997). *Analysis of incomplete multivariate data*. New York: Chapman & Hall.

Sennott, C., & Mollborn, S. (2011). College-bound teens' decisions about the transition to sex: Negotiating competing norms. *Advances in Life Course Research, 16*, 83–97. doi:10.1016/j.alcr.2011.05.001

Shaw, L. A., Wainryb, C., & Smetana, J. (2014). Early and middle adolescents' reasoning about moral and personal concerns in opposite-sex interactions. *Social Development, 23*, 784–802. doi:10.1111/sode.12076

Small, S., & Luster, T. (1994). Adolescent sexual activity: An ecological, risk-factor approach. *Journal of Marriage and the Family, 56*, 181–192. doi:10.2307/352712

Smetana, J. G. (1995). Parenting styles and conceptions of parental authority during adolescence. *Child Development, 66*, 299–316. doi:10.2307/1131579

Smetana, J. G. (2006). Social domain theory: Consistencies and variations in children's moral and social judgments. In M. Killen & J. G. Smetana (Eds.), *Handbook of moral development* (pp. 119–154). Mahwah, NJ: Erlbaum.

Soenens, B., Beyers, W., Vansteenkiste, M., Sierens, E., Luyckx, K., & Goossens, L. (2004). *The 'gross anatomy' of parenting styles in adolescence: Three or four dimensions?* Paper presented at the 18th biennial meeting of the International Society for the Study of Behavioural Development (ISSBD), Ghent, Belgium.

Soenens, B., Vansteenkiste, M., Smits, I., Lowet, K., & Goossens, L. (2007). The role of intrusive parenting in the relationship between peer management strategies and peer affiliation. *Journal of Applied Developmental Psychology, 28*, 239–249. doi:10.1016/j.appdev.2007.02.003

Steinberg, L. (2001). We know some things: Parent–adolescent relationships in retrospect and prospect. *Journal of Research on Adolescence, 11*, 1–19. doi:10.1111/1532-7795.00001

Steinberg, L., & Monahan, K. C. (2007). Age differences in resistance to peer influence. *Developmental Psychology, 43*, 1531–1543. doi:10.1037/0012-1649.43.6.1531

Tilton-Weaver, L. C., & Galambos, N. L. (2003). Adolescents' characteristics and parents' beliefs as predictors of parents' peer management behaviors. *Journal of Research on Adolescence, 13*, 269–300. doi:10.1111/1532-7795.1303002

Treboux, D., & Busch-Rossnagel, N. A. (1995). Age differences in parent and peer influences on female sexual behavior. *Journal of Research on Adolescence, 5*, 469–487. doi:10.1207/s15327795jra0504_5

Van de Bongardt, D., de Graaf, H., Reitz, E., & Deković, M. (2014). Parents as moderators of longitudinal associations between sexual peer norms and Dutch adolescents' sexual initiation and intention. *Journal of Adolescent Health, 55*, 388–393. doi:10.1016/j.jadohealth.2014.02.017

Van de Bongardt, D., Reitz, E., & Deković, M. (2012). Vroeg seksueel debuut in Nederland: Een longitudinale studie naar de rol van individuele kenmerken, opvoeding en leeftijdgenoten. *Kind en Adolescent, 33*, 194–205. doi:10.1007/s12453-012-0026-0

Van de Bongardt, D., Reitz, E., Sandfort, T., & Deković, M. (2014). A meta-analysis of the relations between three types of peer norms and adolescent sexual behavior. *Personality and Social Psychology Review*. doi:10.1177/1088868314544223

Whitaker, D. J., & Miller, K. S. (2000). Parent–adolescent discussions about sex and condoms: Impact on peer influences of sexual risk behavior. *Journal of Adolescent Research, 15*, 251–273. doi:10.1177/0743558400152004

White, C. N., & Warner, L. A. (2015). Influence of family and school-level factors on age of sexual initiation. *Journal of Adolescent Health, 56*, 231–237. doi:10.1016/j.jadohealth.2014.09.017

Project STARS (Studies on Trajectories of Adolescent Relationships and Sexuality): A longitudinal, multi-domain study on sexual development of Dutch adolescents

Ellen Reitz[1], Daphne van de Bongardt[1], Laura Baams[1], Suzan Doornwaard[1], Wieke Dalenberg[2], Judith Semon Dubas[1], Marcel van Aken[1], Geertjan Overbeek[3], Tom ter Bogt[1], Regina van der Eijnden[1], Ine Vanwesenbeeck[1], Saskia Kunnen[2], Greetje Timmerman[2], Paul van Geert[2], and Maja Deković[1]

[1]Utrecht University, Utrecht, The Netherlands
[2]University of Groningen, Groningen, The Netherlands
[3]University of Amsterdam, Amsterdam, The Netherlands

This study gives an overview of Project STARS (Studies on Trajectories of Adolescent Relationships and Sexuality), a four-wave longitudinal study of 1297 Dutch adolescents. First, the sample, measures and four sub-projects are described. Second, hierarchical regression analyses were conducted to examine how key variables from the individual domain (impulsivity), parent domain (parent–adolescent relationship quality), peer domain (involvement with peers) and media domain (time spent on social networking sites), and their interactions predict changes in the experience with sexual behaviour of adolescents across time. Results showed that higher levels of impulsivity, lower quality of relation with parents, more frequent involvement with peers and more time spent on social networking sites at baseline predicted increases in sexual experience of adolescents over a subsequent 1.5-year time period. No interaction effects among the domains were

No potential conflict of interest was reported by the authors.
"Project STARS" (Studies on Trajectories of Adolescent Relationships and Sexuality) is funded by the Dutch Organisation for Scientific Research (NWO) and the Fund for Scientific Research of Sexuality (FWOS) [NWO grant no. 431-99-018].

found. The findings highlight the significance of a multi-domain approach to the study of adolescent sexual development.

As adolescents mature, they gradually engage in sexual behaviours of increasing intimacy, varying from kissing to sexual intercourse (De Graaf, Vanwesenbeeck, Meijer, Woertman, & Meeus, 2009). According to the biosocial model (Udry, 1988) and other ecological models (e.g., Bronfenbrenner, 1979), it is important to consider both individual and socio-contextual domains when investigating developments in adolescents' (sexual) behaviour. Project STARS (Studies on Trajectories of Adolescent Relationships and Sexuality; Deković, Van Aken, Ter Bogt, & Van Geert, 2010) is a prospective four-wave longitudinal study on romantic and sexual development of Dutch adolescents that builds on this ecological perspective. The study includes a focus on individual characteristics as well as proximal (parents, peers) and more distal (media) social domains that are relevant for predicting sexual development during adolescence. Furthermore, whereas most research on adolescent sexuality tends to focus on a narrow definition of sexuality (e.g., the age at first intercourse) with relatively little attention to the full range of behaviours involved in the development of sexuality (e.g., Santelli et al., 2004), Project STARS considers sexual behaviour broadly, ranging from kissing to intercourse. The present study provides an overview of the Project STARS study design and investigates the degree to which individual and social domains predict change in adolescents' experience with sexual behaviour.

PROJECT STARS

Project STARS is unique in its design, including four sub-projects that each address a specific domain that has a role in sexual development. Project 1 focuses on individual characteristics. The project examines for example pubertal development, personality and impulsivity (Baams, Overbeek, Dubas, & van Aken, 2014; Baams et al., 2014). Project 2 investigates parents and peers and interactions between them. The role of both general (e.g., relationship quality) and sexuality-specific (e.g., sexual communication) parenting dimensions is studied (e.g., Van de Bongardt, De Graaf, Reitz, & Deković, 2014). In addition, different types of sexual norms among peers (e.g., peer sexual behaviours and attitudes) are examined (Van de Bongardt, Reitz, Sandfort, & Deković, 2014). Project 3 focuses on both receptive [e.g., the use of sexually explicit Internet material (SEIM)] and interactive [e.g., social networking site use (SNS)] sex-related online behaviours in relation to adolescents' sexual development, as well as the personal and socio-contextual conditions in which these relations are embedded (Doornwaard, Moreno, Van den Eijnden, Vanwesenbeeck, & Ter Bogt, 2014; Doornwaard, Van den Eijnden, Overbeek, &

Ter Bogt, 2014). Project 4 uses semi-structured qualitative diaries to zoom in on adolescents' subjective perceptions of romantic and sexual behaviours in daily life. The focus is on an elaborated definition of sexuality that includes covert thoughts and fantasies and romantic topics, in addition to overt behaviours and explicit sex-related content (Dalenberg, Timmerman, Kunnen, & Van Geert, 2015; Dalenberg, Timmerman, Van Geert, & Kunnen, 2015). Combined, the aim of the four sub-projects is to examine the importance of individual characteristics and social domains in relation to adolescent sexual development both separately and in interaction with each other.

Design

Project STARS is a four-wave longitudinal study that began in the Fall of 2011 and followed a sample of adolescents an additional three times at 6-month intervals. Participants (1297 Dutch adolescents between 10 and 18 years (mean age = 13.67; SD = 1.36), 53.3% boys) were recruited from eight elementary ($n = 165$) and four secondary ($n = 1132$) schools in large cities and small municipalities throughout the Netherlands. The longitudinal sample represents five age cohorts of adolescents in five consecutive grades: the last year of elementary school (6th grade) and the first 4 years of secondary school (7th–10th grade). A total of 872 (67.2%) participants had complete data (four waves); 227 (17.5%) had data on three waves, and 154 (11.9%) had data on two waves. The majority of the sample had a Dutch (73.6%) or other Western (10.1%) ethnic background.

Before the first measurement, eligible adolescents and their parents received information describing the aims of the study, confidentiality safeguards and procedures for declining or ending participation. Of the approached adolescents, 9.2% decided not to participate or were not allowed by their parents to take part in the study. Adolescents completed a diverse battery of psychological and sociological measures designed to assess individual and relational characteristics of the adolescents as well as those of parents, peers, and Internet use.[1] Adolescents completed these questionnaires online using computers at their school, during regular school hours. Researchers and trained research assistants were present to supervise the data collection. Adolescents received book certificates of increasing values after each completed questionnaire.

In order to curb the length of the extensive online questionnaire, and to minimize potential data loss due to weariness, we limited the number of items for several concepts in the questionnaire with the use of a planned missingness design (Graham, Taylor, Olchowski, & Cumsille, 2006). In this design, participants were randomly assigned to one of three groups, which completed a different

[1]For a complete list of measures, the Project STARS Scale book can be requested from the researchers.

combination of items from the original scale (e.g., for a six-item scale, three items were completed by all groups, and each group completed an additional randomly selected item). This design was used only at T1 and T2; at T3 and T4 all items in the questionnaire were assessed. Missing items were subsequently imputed using multiple imputation (MI; Schafer & Graham, 2002) or expectation-maximization estimation (EM; Dempster, Laird, & Rubin, 1977) in SPSS, version 20 (SPSS Inc., Chicago, IL), or using full information maximum likelihood (FIML) in Mplus (Los Angeles, CA, USA) (Muthén & Muthén, 1998–2012).

THE ROLE OF INDIVIDUAL AND SOCIAL DOMAINS ON THE EXPERIENCE WITH SEXUAL BEHAVIOUR OF ADOLESCENTS

Project STARS provides us with the opportunity to investigate predictors of adolescent sexual development from multiple domains. In this study, we investigated one key variable from each of the four domains that have been consistently related to adolescent sexual behaviour. Within the individual domain, impulsivity is a personality trait that affects various aspects of adolescents' functioning (Blaszczynski, Steel, & McConaghy, 1997) and is often studied in relation to sexual behaviour. For example, higher impulsivity is related with an earlier age of first sexual intercourse, a higher number of sexual partners, more unprotected sex and a higher risk of contracting a sexually transmitted infection (De Daas, Hafner, & De Wit, 2014).

Regarding the social domain, the parent and peer domains are two of the most proximal and influential social domains in youth's lives (e.g., Szapocznik & Coatsworth, 1999). As a general aspect of parenting, the quality of adolescents' relationship with their parents (i.e., the level of warmth, closeness and support) is widely examined in relation with adolescent sexual behaviour and is consistently related to delayed sexual activity (e.g., De Graaf, Vanwesenbeeck, Woertman, & Meeus, 2011; Lenciauskiene & Zaborskis, 2008). In the peer context, a high degree of peer involvement has often been linked to adolescents' sexuality. For example, adolescents who spent more time with peers tend to be more sexually active (e.g., Barnes, Hoffman, Welte, Farrell, & Dintcheff, 2007).

In addition to these proximal domains, another domain that is highly relevant for adolescents' developing sexuality is the Internet. Social networking sites such as Facebook and Twitter are very popular among adolescents (Lenhart, Purcell, Smith, & Zickuhr, 2010) and they aid not only in creating an identity but also in forming romantic relationships and the development of a sexual self (Doornwaard et al., 2014). Sexual content is part of many adolescents' social networking profiles (Moreno et al., 2009), and these sites may function as a media "superpeer", promoting (sexual) behavioural norms among other adolescents (Strasburger & Wilson, 2002). It might therefore be expected that adolescents who spent much time on social networking sites would also show high levels of experience with sexual behaviour.

Although many studies link either the individual domain or social domains to sexual behaviour of adolescents, only a limited number of studies examined how multiple domains operate together to either promote or delay sexual behaviour (e.g., Boislard & Poulin, 2011; Friedlander, Connolly, Pepler, & Craig, 2007). These studies usually included two or three domains such as the individual, parent and peer domain, without consideration of the role of media/Internet. To the best of our knowledge, only one study has previously examined multiple domains, including religion, parents, peers, school and mass media, in predicting sexual intention and behaviour (L'Engle, Brown, & Kenneavy, 2006). The strongest predictor was peer sexual behaviour, although parental relationship quality and media use were also significant. In this study, however, mass media included television, CDs, movies and magazines, but not Internet use. Thus, despite increasing research on the role of Internet use in adolescent sexual development, this domain has not yet been compared to other domains in a comprehensive model. The present study is unique in that it includes the individual, parent, peer as well as the Internet domain.

In this study we examined how each of these domains predicted changes in experience with sexual behaviour over the course of 18 months. We expected that higher levels of impulsivity, involvement with peers, and time spent on social networking sites and a poorer relation with parents would be associated with more experience with sexual behaviour. On the basis of previous research (Boislard & Poulin, 2011; Friedlander et al., 2007; L'Engle et al., 2006), we expected that the individual and peer domain would be particularly strongly linked to experience with sexual behaviour.

In addition to the relative strength of different domains, ecological models posit that individual and contextual domains interact with each other in influencing behaviour (e.g., Bronfenbrenner, 1979). In this study, we tested all six possible interactions among domains. Although studies investigating interactions between different domains on adolescent sexual behaviour are scarce, some studies exhibit interactions between parents and peers in predicting adolescent sexual behaviour, showing that parents can buffer the effects of peers (Fasula & Miller, 2006; Whitaker & Miller, 2000). On the basis of these studies, we expected that a high quality of the parent–adolescent relationship would decrease the effect of involvement of peers on experience with sexual behaviour. Taking into account the novelty of testing interaction effects regarding sexual behaviour, we consider the other interactions to be exploratory.

METHOD

Participants

For this study, we selected adolescents who were attending secondary school ($n = 1132$), as the questionnaire for the younger elementary school children did not include all investigated instruments. Table 1 presents the demographic

TABLE 1
Descriptives of demographic variables of the present study at Time 1

Demographics	*Present study*
N	1132
Mean age (SD)	13.96 (1.18)
Age range	11–18
% Boys	52.7
Ethnic background	
% Dutch	79.2
% Western	11.0
% Non-Western	9.8
Educational level	
n lower education[a]	430
n higher education[b]	640

[a]Preparatory secondary vocational education programmes.
[b]Higher general continued or preparatory scientific education programmes.

characteristics of this sample. Data from the first and last waves were used in the analyses (1.5 years in between).

Instruments

Experience with sexual behaviour. To assess experience with sexual behaviour, adolescents were first asked two questions: "Have you ever French kissed somebody?" and "Have you ever had sex with another person? With sex we mean everything from touching or caressing to intercourse", answered with 0 = *no* or 1 = *yes*. Adolescents who indicated *yes* on the second question received follow-up questions about their experience with different sexual behaviours: naked touching or caressing, performing or receiving manual sex, performing or receiving oral sex and vaginal or anal intercourse (0 = *no*; 1 = *yes*). These items were combined into one variable measuring the level of adolescents' experience with sexual behaviour, ranging from 0 = *no experience with any behaviours* to 5 = *experience with all behaviours* ($\alpha_{\text{Time1}} = .78$; $\alpha_{\text{Time4}} = .86$).

Impulsivity. Impulsivity was measured with the Eysenck Impulsiveness Scale (Vitaro, Arseneault, & Tremblay, 1997). Adolescents reported on five items (e.g., "Mostly I do or say things without thinking about it") to which extend they agreed with it or not, ranging from 1 = *completely not agree* to 5 = *completely agree.* Higher scores indicated higher levels of impulsivity ($\alpha_{\text{Time1}} = .74$). For this scale a planned missingness design was used and missing values were imputed using MI.

Relationship quality with parents. The quality of adolescents' relationship with their parents was measured with the Network of Relationship Inventory (NRI; Furman & Buhrmester, 2009). Adolescents chose to complete items for their mother ($n = 1065$) or father ($n = 151$), based on their selection of which parent spent most time with them and had most caring tasks for them. Answers for mothers and fathers were then combined in one parent variable. The scale consisted of six items that measured levels of satisfaction (three items: e.g., "How satisfied are you with your relationship with your [choice parent]?") and conflict (three items: e.g., "How often do you and your [choice parent] argue with each other?") within the relationship. Answers ranged from 1 = *none* to 5 = *the most*. The correlation between the two scales was $r = .40$. Items from the conflict scale were recoded and the two scales were combined to create a total parent–adolescent relationship quality scale, in which higher scores indicated a higher quality ($\alpha_{Time1} = .85$).

Involvement with peers. The degree of involvement with peers was measured with five items based on several studies (Kandel & Davies, 1982; Simpson & McBride, 1992; Sieving, Eisenberg, Pettingell, & Skay, 2006). Adolescents were asked to indicate on a six-point scale, ranging from 1 = *never* to 6 = *very often*, how often they: meet their friends after school, meet at a friend's house, go to a party with friends, talk with friends about their problems and talk with friends on the phone. Higher scores indicated more frequent involvement with peers ($\alpha_{Time1} = .74$). For this scale a planned missingness design was used and missing values were imputed using MI.

Time spent on social networking sites. To assess the time spent on social networking sites, adolescents were first asked whether they have a social networking site or profile page, which could be answered with 0 = *no* or 1 = *yes*. Adolescents who indicated *yes* (86.6%) received a follow-up question asking how much time per day they spend on this social networking site, with answers ranging from 1 = *less than 15 min* to 6 = *more than 4 h*. Adolescents who answered the first question with *no* (6.7%) received a score of "0" on this variable. Higher scores indicated more time spent on social networking sites.

Analyses

Given that sexual behaviour is related to age, gender, educational level and ethnicity, these variables were included as control variables in the analyses. To test our hypothesis that each domain (individual, parent, peer and media) at Time 1 would uniquely predict experience with sexual behaviour of adolescents at Time 4, hierarchical regression analyses were performed. On the first step, Time 1 experience with sexual behaviour was entered along with the control variables. On the second step, impulsivity, parent–adolescent relationship quality, peer involvement and time spent on social networking sites were entered. On the third step, the six interaction terms were entered. Because planned missingness was used for several variables in the project, the items from these scales were imputed with MI (across five sets). Only pooled B-values were given in the regression analyses (not betas). Because B-values are dependent on the measurement scale, all variables were standardized before inclusion in the regression analyses, making comparisons between variables possible.

RESULTS

Our longitudinal design allowed us to check over-time inconsistencies regarding adolescents' reports on experience with sexual behaviour. A total of 16 adolescents were excluded from the analyses (e.g., adolescents scoring "2" on T1, "4" on T2, "3" on T3, and "1" on T4), whereas a total of 47 adolescents with a missing value on T1 or T4 were additionally included on the basis of their longitudinal scores (e.g., adolescents who had a missing value on T1 and a "0" on all other waves. The missing value on T1 was replaced with "0").

Table 2 shows intercorrelations and means of the key variables. The rank-order stability of adolescent sexuality was high across the 18-month period. Adolescents' levels of experience with sexual behaviour increased significantly from T1 to T4 ($t\,(894) = 16.44, p = .000$). All domains were significantly related to experience with sexual behaviour, both cross-sectionally and longitudinally. Specifically, higher levels of impulsivity, more frequent involvement with peers and more time spent on social networking sites were related to more experience with sexual behaviour, whereas a higher parent–adolescent relationship quality was related to less experience with sexual behaviour. The four domains showed relatively low intercorrelations (*rs* ranging between .24 and .30), suggesting that

TABLE 2
Intercorrelations, means, and standard deviations (SD) of assessed variables

	1	*2*	*3*	*4*	*5*	*6*
1. Sexual behaviour T1	–					
2. Sexual behaviour T4	.70***	–				
3. Impulsivity T1	.14***	.22***	–			
4. Relationship parents T1	−.16***	−.23***	−.24***	–		
5. Involvement peers T1	.33***	.34***	.11**	−.00	–	
6. Time spent SNS T1	.22***	.30***	.23***	−.17***	.30***	–
Means	0.62	1.14	2.67	4.63	3.66	2.63
SD	1.10	1.60	.79	.72	.93	1.50

Notes: SNS = social networking site. *N* ranges from 924 to 1075.
$^{**}p < .01$. $^{***}p < .001$

they were rather independent from each other. Regarding the mean values observed, adolescents were—on average—initially sexually inexperienced (0.62 on a 0 to 5 scale), enjoyed very good relationships with their parents (4.63 on a 1 to 5 scale), were moderately involved with their peers (3.66 on a 1 to 6 scale) and spent a moderate amount of time on social networking sites (2.63 on a 0 to 6 scale).

Table 3 (Model a) reports the results of the hierarchical regression analysis that includes the covariates and the main effect of the four domains. As expected, the previous level of experience with sexual behaviour was the strongest predictor of subsequent sexual experience. Moreover, age and educational level were significant covariates: older adolescents and adolescents with lower educational levels reported more experience with sexual behaviour at T4 than younger adolescents and adolescents with higher educational levels. Gender and ethnicity did not significantly account for differences in experience with sexual behaviour.

TABLE 3

Linear regression analyses predicting experience with sexual behaviour (T4) from individual, parenting, peer, and media domains (T1)

		Sexual behaviour T4			
		Model a		*Model b*	
Step		*B*	*Δ R^2*	*B*	*Δ R^2*
1	*Control variables*		.52***		.52***
	Gender[a]	.00		.00	
	Age	.11***		.11***	
	Education	−.03**		−.03**	
	Ethnicity[b]	.06		.05	
	Sexual behaviour T1	.62***		.62***	
2	*Domains*		.05***		.05***
	Impulsivity T1	.07*		.07*	
	Relationship parents T1	−.09**		−.08**	
	Involvement peers T1	.12***		.13***	
	Time spent SNS T1	.11***		.11***	
3	*Interactions among domains*				.00
	Impulsivity × Relationship parents			−.00	
	Impulsivity × Involvement peers			.02	
	Impulsivity × Time spent SNS			−.01	
	Relationship parents × Involvement peers			−.02	
	Relationship parents × Time spent SNS			−.04	
	Involvement peers × Time spent SNS			.02	

Notes: Model a includes only the first two steps in the analysis, whereas Model b also includes interactions among domains. SNS = social networking site.

[a]0 = boys, 1 = girls. [b]0 = Western, 1 = non-Western.

*$p < .05$. **$p < .01$. ***$p < .001$.

Regarding the substantive multi-domain predictors, higher levels of impulsivity, more frequent involvement with peers and more time spent on social networking sites at T1 predicted increases in experience with sexual behaviour from T1 to T4, whereas higher levels of parent–adolescent relationship quality at T1 predicted fewer changes in experience with sexual behaviour from T1 to T4.

In the next step, we added the six two-way interaction effects between the four domains in predicting adolescents' experience with sexual behaviour (see Table 3, Model b). The results showed that none of these interactions were significant ($p > .05$).

DISCUSSION

This study described Project STARS, the first large-scale longitudinal study in the Netherlands that examines sexual development during adolescence in relation to multiple domains. Consistent with previous studies, adolescents who were more impulsive (De Daas et al., 2014) reported a lower relationship quality with their parents (De Graaf et al., 2011; Lenciauskiene & Zaborskis, 2008), and spent more time with their peers (Barnes et al., 2007) showed more increases in experience with sexual behaviour (i.e., reported experience with more different sexual behaviours) over time. Moreover, results confirmed our expectation that more time spent on social networking sites increased experience with sexual behaviour. Although studies indicated that the individual and peer domains might be better predictors of adolescent sexual activity compared to the parent domain (Boislard & Poulin, 2011; Friedlander et al., 2007) or the media domain (L'Engle et al., 2006), the present study shows that all four domains were relevant. To the best of our knowledge, this study is the first that incorporates multiple domains with the inclusion of adolescents' Internet use. The finding that both involvement with peers and time spent on social networking sites were related to increases in experience with sexual behaviour suggests that peers are important socializing agents, both offline and online. Peer norms play an important role in adolescents' own sexual behaviour (e.g., Van de Bongardt et al., 2014), and social networking sites provide opportunities to convey these peer norms online. This seems to support the suggestion that social networking sites can act as a "superpeer" in shaping sexual behaviour (Strasburger & Wilson, 2002). Thus, it seems important to study not only relations with peers offline but also online.

None of the tested interactions were significant. Owing to their exploratory nature, only one hypothesis was formulated: we expected that parents would decrease the effects of peers on experience with sexual behaviour, in line with previous studies (Fasula & Miller, 2006; Whitaker & Miller, 2000). An explanation for the fact that moderating effects were not found in the present study might be that we used only general parent and peer measures instead of sexuality-specific measures. Studies that investigated sexuality-specific measures showed moderating effects of mother's responsiveness during sex discussions on the relationship between peer sexual activity and sexual intercourse (Fasula & Miller, 2006), and moderating effects of parental communication about sex/condoms on the relationship between peer norms for sexual activity/condom use and sexual behaviour (Whitaker & Miller, 2000). This suggests that it seems important for future studies to explore interactions between general and sexual-specific measures or between sexual-specific measures only to examine their effect on sexual behaviour.

The present study is the first that longitudinally examined how multiple domains predict changes in experience with sexual behaviour using a large sample of adolescents with a broad age range. Nonetheless, findings have to be interpreted with a number of limitations in mind. First, despite our efforts to include adolescents with different ethnic backgrounds, the secondary school sample consists of a fairly large group of Western adolescents (90.2%) compared to the general Dutch population (84%) (Statistics Netherlands, 2013), which does not allow us to generalize results to adolescents with different ethnic backgrounds. Furthermore, the Project STARS sample is a relatively homogeneous sample with, due to their young age, low levels of sexual experience. Also, the sample is highly satisfied with their relationship with their parents, moderately involved with peers and spent a moderate amount of time on social networking sites, imposing limits on the generalizability of the findings.

Second, all measures examined in this study were derived from adolescent self-reports. Although adolescents may not provide accurate reports about their experience with sexual behaviour (Brener, Billy, & Grady, 2003), adolescent self-reports seem the best method to collect data on sexual behaviour, considering the private nature of this behaviour. Our longitudinal design allowed us to check the over-time validity of the self-reported sexual behaviours and to exclude adolescents ($n = 16$) with inconsistent reports about their sexual behaviour. Regarding the parent–adolescent relationship quality, adolescents' perceptions of parenting have been found to be more predictive of their sexual behaviour than parent reports (Jaccard, Dittus, & Gordon, 1998). In addition, the level of contact with peers is difficult to determine without asking adolescents themselves, because most contact with peers usually happens outside of direct adult supervision (Laird, Pettit, Dodge, & Bates, 1999). Finally, adolescents have easy online access through multiple devices throughout the day, and are most capable in estimating the time they spent on social networking sites themselves.

Notwithstanding these limitations, the results highlight the significance of a multi-domain approach to the study of adolescent sexual development, in line with ecological models (e.g., Bronfenbrenner, 1979). Findings showed that experience with sexual behaviour is part of a broader context, and that knowledge of this broader context is significant for a better understanding of youth' sexuality. Taking such a multi-domain perspective is important for three reasons. First, it contributes to a more detailed theoretical understanding of sexual development during adolescence. Second, it guides future studies on adolescent sexual development in their design and focus. Third, it aids in the development and improvement of prevention and intervention strategies that are aimed at promoting a healthy sexual development. Project STARS provides the opportunity to take this perspective and, in addition, the four sub-projects each provide more in-depth knowledge in the importance of the different domains in which adolescent sexuality develops.

REFERENCES

Baams, L., Overbeek, G., Dubas, J. S., & van Aken, M. A. (2014). On early starters and late bloomers: The development of sexual behavior in adolescence across personality types. *The Journal of Sex Research, 51*, 754–764. doi:10.1080/00224499.2013.802758

Baams, L., Overbeek, G., Van de Bongardt, D., Reitz, E., Dubas, J. S., & van Aken, M. A. G. (2014). Adolescents' and their friends' sexual behavior and intention: Selection effects of personality type. *Journal of Research in Personality*. Advance online publication. doi:10.1016/j.jrp.2014.07.009

Barnes, G. M., Hoffman, J. H., Welte, J. W., Farrell, M. P., & Dintcheff, B. A. (2007). Adolescents' time use: Effects on substance use, delinquency and sexual activity. *Journal of Youth and Adolescence, 36*, 697–710. doi:10.1007/s10964-006-9075-0

Blaszczynski, A., Steel, Z., & McConaghy, N. (1997). Impulsivity in pathological gambling: The antisocial impulsivist. *Addiction, 92*, 75–87. doi:10.1111/j.1360-0443.1997.tb03639.x

Boislard, P. M. A., & Poulin, F. (2011). Individual, familial, friends-related and contextual predictors of early sexual intercourse. *Journal of Adolescence, 34*, 289–300. doi:10.1016/j.adolescence.2010.05.002

Brener, N. D., Billy, J. O. G., & Grady, W. R. (2003). Assessment of factors affecting the validity of self-reported health-risk behavior among adolescents: Evidence from the scientific literature. *Journal of Adolescent Health, 33*, 436–457. doi:10.1016/S1054-139X(03)00052-1

Bronfenbrenner, U. (1979). *The ecology of human development: Experiments by nature and design*. Cambridge, MA: Harvard University Press.

Dalenberg, W., Timmerman, G., Kunnen, S., & Van Geert, P. (2015). *Adolescents' romantic and sexual behavior: Snapshots from everyday life. A one-time qualitative diary method*. Manuscript in preparation.

Dalenberg, W., Timmerman, G., Van Geert, P., & Kunnen, S. (2015). *"Let's talk about something else". A qualitative diary study of adolescents' experiences of romance and sexuality and parent–adolescent conversations*. Manuscript submitted for publication.

De Daas, C., Hafner, M., & De Wit, J. (2014). The impact of long-term health goals on sexual risk decisions in impulsive and reflective cognitive states. *Archives of Sexual Behavior, 43*, 659–667. doi:10.1007/s10508-013-0183-0

De Graaf, H., Vanwesenbeeck, I., Meijer, S., Woertman, L., & Meeus, W. (2009). Sexual trajectories during adolescence: Relation to demographic characteristics and sexual risk. *Archives of Sexual Behavior, 38*, 276–282.

De Graaf, H., Vanwesenbeeck, I., Woertman, L., & Meeus, W. (2011). Parenting and adolescents' sexual development in Western societies. *European Psychologist, 16*, 21–31. doi:10.1027/1016-9040/a000031

Deković, M., Van Aken, M. A. G., Ter Bogt, T. F. M., & Van Geert, P. (2010). *Sexuality and intimate relations of Dutch youth: Developmental trajectories and developmental context (Project STARS).* (Netherlands Organization for Scientific Research (NWO) Grant no. 431-99-018). Unpublished Manuscript.

Dempster, A. P., Laird, N. M., & Rubin, D. B. (1977). Maximum likelihood estimation from incomplete data via the EM algorithm (with discussion). *Journal of the Royal Statistical Society, B39*, 1–38.

Doornwaard, S. M., Moreno, M. A., Van den Eijnden, R. J. J. M., Vanwesenbeeck, I., & Ter Bogt, T. F. M. (2014). Young adolescents' sexual and romantic reference displays on Facebook. *Journal of Adolescent Health, 55*, 535–541. doi:10.1016/j.jadohealth.2014.04.002

Doornwaard, S. M., Van den Eijnden, R. J. J. M., Overbeek, G. J., & Ter Bogt, T. F. M. (2014). Differential developmental profiles of adolescents using sexually explicit Internet material. *Journal of Sex Research.* Advance online publication. doi:10.1080/00224499.2013.866195

Fasula, A. M., & Miller, K. S. (2006). African-American and Hispanic adolescents' intentions to delay first intercourse: Parental communication as a buffer for sexually active peers. *Journal of Adolescent Health, 38*, 193–200. doi:10.1016/j.jadohealth.2004.12.009

Friedlander, L. J., Connolly, J. A., Pepler, D. J., & Craig, W. M. (2007). Biological, familial, and peer influences on dating in early adolescence. *Archives of Sexual Behavior, 36*, 821–830. doi:10.1007/s10508-006-9130-7

Furman, W, & Buhrmester, D. (2009). Methods and measures: The Network of Relationships Inventory: Behavioral systems version. *International Journal of Behavioral Development, 33*, 470–478. doi:10.1177/0165025409342634

Graham, J. W., Taylor, B. J., Olchowski, A. E., & Cumsille, P. E. (2006). Planned missing data designs in psychological research. *Psychological Methods, 11*, 323–343. doi:10.1037/1082-989X.11.4.323

Jaccard, J., Dittus, P. J., & Gordon, V. V. (1998). Parent-adolescent congruency in reports of adolescent sexual behavior and in communications about sexual behavior. *Child Development, 69*, 247–261. doi:10.1111/j.1467-8624.1998.tb06146.x

Kandel, D., & Davies, M. (1982). Epidemiology of depressive mood in adolescents. *Archives of General Psychiatry, 39*, 1205–1212. doi:10.1001/archpsyc.1982.04290100065011

Laird, R. D., Pettit, G. S., Dodge, K. A., & Bates, J. E. (1999). Best friendships, group relationships, and antisocial behavior in early adolescence. *Journal of Early Adolescence, 19*, 413–437. doi:10.1177/0272431699019004001

Lenciauskiene, I., & Zaborskis, A. (2008). The effects of family structure, parent–child relationship and parental monitoring on early sexual behaviour among adolescents in nine European countries. *Scandinavian Journal of Public Health, 36*, 607–618. doi:10.1177/1403494807088460

L'Engle, K. L., Brown, J. D., & Kenneavy, K (2006). The mass media are an important context for adolescents' sexual behavior. *Journal of Adolescent Health, 38*, 186–192. doi:10.1016/j.jadohealth.2005.03.020

Lenhart, A., Purcell, K., Smith, A., & Zickuhr, K. (2010). *Social media and young adults.* Washington, DC: Pew Internet & American Life Project.

Moreno, M. A., Parks, M. R., Zimmerman, F. J., Brito, T. E., & Christakis, D. A. (2009). Display of health risk behaviors on MySpace by adolescents: Prevalence and associations. *Archives of Pediatrics and Adolescent Medicine, 163*, 27–34. doi:10.1001/archpediatrics.2008.528

Muthén, L. K., & Muthén, B. O. (1998–2012). *Mplus user's guide* (7th ed.). Los Angeles, CA: Muthén & Muthén.

Santelli, J. S., Kaiser, J., Hirsch, L., Radosh, A., Simkin, L., & Middlestadt, S. (2004). Initiation of sexual intercourse among middle school adolescents: The influence of psychosocial factors. *Journal of Adolescent Health, 34*, 200–208. doi:10.1016/j.jadohealth.2003.06.004

Schafer, J. L., & Graham, J. W. (2002). Missing data: our view of the state of the art. *Psychological Methods, 7*, 147–177. doi:10.1037/1082-989X.7.2.147

Sieving, R. E., Eisenberg, M. E., Pettingell, S., & Skay, C. (2006). Friends' influence on adolescents' first sexual intercourse. *Perspectives on Sexual and Reproductive Health, 38*, 13–19. doi:10.1363/3801306

Simpson, D. D., & McBride, A. A. (1992). Family, friends, and self (FFS) assessment scales for Mexican American youth. *Hispanic Journal of Behavioral Sciences, 14*, 327–340. doi:10.1177/07399863920143003

Statistics Netherlands. (2013). Statline: Population 2013. Retrieved from http://statline.cbs.nl

Strasburger, V. C., & Wilson, B. J. (2002). *Children, adolescents and the media.* Beverly Hills, CA: Sage.

Szapocznik, J., & Coatsworth, J. D. (1999). An ecodevelopmental framework for organizing risk and protection for drug abuse: A developmental model of risk and protection. In M. Glantz & C. R. Hartel (Eds.), *Drug abuse: Origins and interventions* (pp. 331–366). Washington, DC: American Psychological Association.

Udry, J. R. (1988). Biological predispositions and social control in adolescent sexual behavior. *American Sociological Review, 53*, 709–722. doi:10.2307/2095817

Van de Bongardt, D., De Graaf, H., Reitz, E., & Deković, M. (2014). Parents as moderators of longitudinal associations between sexual peer norms and Dutch adolescents' sexual initiation and intention. *Journal of Adolescent Health, 55*, 388–393. doi:10.1016/j.jadohealth.2014.02.017

Van de Bongardt, D., Reitz, E., Sandfort, Th. G. M., & Deković, M. (2014). A meta-analysis of the relations between three types of peer norms and adolescent sexual behavior. *Personality and Social Psychology Review*. Advance online publication. doi:10.1177/1088868314544223

Vitaro, F., Arseneault, L., & Tremblay, R. E. (1997). Dispositional predictors of problem gambling in male adolescents. *American Journal of Psychiatry, 154*, 1769–1770. doi:10.1176/ajp.154.12.1769

Whitaker, D., & Miller, K. (2000). Parent-adolescent discussions about sex and condoms: Impact on peer influences of sexual risk behavior. *Journal of Adolescent Research, 15*, 251–273.

Index

For Product Safety Concerns and Information please contact our EU representative GPSR@taylorandfrancis.com Taylor & Francis Verlag GmbH, Kaufingerstraße 24, 80331 München, Germany

Batch number: 10725973

Printed by Printforce, the Netherlands